The Philosophy of Love:

Bridging Western, Eastern and Arabic Thought

The Philosophy of Love:

Bridging Western, Eastern and Arabic Thought

Joyce Åkesson

Pallas Athena Distribution

Lund 2025

The Philosophy of Love: Bridging Western, Eastern and Arabic Thought
By Joyce Åkesson

ISBN: 978-91-989454-6-1

CONTENTS

Preface

Defining love is a complex endeavour, as it encompasses a wide array of emotions, experiences, and expressions that vary across cultures and individuals. At its core, love can be viewed as a profound affection toward someone or something, characterised by feelings of warmth, attachment, and deep care. This emotional bond can manifest in numerous forms, including romantic love, familial love, platonic love, and even self-love. Each of these types carries its own nuances and significance, shaping how individuals connect with one another and interpret their experiences.

Communication plays a pivotal role in the expression and understanding of love. Love languages highlight the ways individuals express and receive love, including words of affirmation, acts of service, receiving gifts, quality time, and physical touch. Recognising one's love language and that of a partner can enhance communication and deepen connections in romantic relationships. Effective communication fosters intimacy and understanding, enabling partners to navigate challenges and nurture their bond through shared expressions of love.

Love has been a central and multifaceted theme in philosophy, engaging thinkers from antiquity to the present in debates about its nature, value, and role in human life. Many Western, Eastern and Arab philosophers have not only sought to define what love is but have also explored its ethical, metaphysical, and existential dimensions.

The intersection of love and spirituality warrants examination, as many individuals find that their understanding of love is deeply intertwined with their spiritual beliefs. Many spiritual traditions emphasise love as a fundamental principle, often associating it with concepts of compassion, forgiveness, and unity. This spiritual dimension of love can provide a sense of purpose and fulfilment, guiding individuals in their relationships and interactions with others. Exploring love through this lens allows for a richer understanding of its transformative power and the ways it can lead to personal growth and a deeper connection to the world around us.

Ultimately, love remains an ever-evolving concept, central to the human experience. It is a source of immense joy and profound pain, driving creativity, connection, and growth. Its essence is beautifully captured in the timeless words of Rumi:

"Let yourself be silently drawn by the strange pull of what you really love. It will not lead you astray."

Chapter I: Love in Ancient Western Philosophy

Love has been a central theme in ancient Western philosophy, explored by thinkers who sought to understand its nature, purpose, and role in human life. From the poetic musings of early Greek thought to the systematic inquiries of Plato (d. 348/347 BC) and Aristotle (d. 322 BC), love was not merely an emotion but a profound force shaping ethics, metaphysics, and human relationships.

I.1 Plato's Love *(Eros* and the *Ladder of Love)*

Plato's concept of love, particularly as presented in his dialogue *Symposium,* revolves around the idea of *Eros* (erotic love) and the *Ladder of Love,* a metaphorical ascent toward the ultimate appreciation of beauty and wisdom. Unlike modern conceptions of romantic love, Plato's notion of love is deeply philosophical and aims at intellectual and spiritual transcendence rather than mere physical attraction.

Eros in Plato's Philosophy

Eros, in Greek thought, is often associated with passionate and desirous love, but for Plato, it is much more than mere physical attraction. In *Symposium,* he presents love as a powerful force that drives individuals toward the pursuit of truth, beauty, and ultimately, the divine. According to Plato, love is:

• *A desire for the good and the beautiful* – Love is a longing for what we lack, and through love, we seek completion and fulfilment.

• *A transformative force* – Love elevates the soul from bodily pleasures to higher intellectual and spiritual aspirations.

• *Not purely physical* – While physical attraction may initiate love, its ultimate goal is wisdom and the contemplation of absolute beauty.

The Ladder of Love

Plato's *Ladder of Love,* described by Socrates through the words of the priestess Diotima, represents the journey from physical attraction to divine enlightenment. It consists of several ascending stages:

Step 1: Love of a Particular Body

At the most basic level, love begins with physical attraction to a beautiful body. This stage is driven by desire and the pleasures of the senses. However, Plato suggests that this is only the starting point, not the ultimate goal.

Step 2: Love of All Beautiful Bodies

The lover realizes that physical beauty is not unique to one person; it exists in many. At this stage, attraction becomes less about a single individual and more about beauty in general.

Step 3: Love of Beautiful Souls

As the lover matures, they begin to appreciate inner beauty—virtue, character, and intelligence—rather than mere physical appearance. The emphasis shifts from bodily attraction to admiration of the mind and spirit.

Step 4: Love of Laws and Institutions

This stage broadens love beyond individuals to societal virtues, recognising beauty in laws, customs, and moral values that create a just and noble society. Love becomes more intellectual and idealistic.

Step 5: Love of Knowledge

A deeper love emerges for wisdom and philosophy. The lover now seeks truth, knowledge, and intellectual enlightenment, moving beyond personal relationships to a love of learning and discovery.

Step 6: Love of the Form of Beauty (Absolute Beauty)

At the highest level, love transcends all particular instances of beauty and reaches an appreciation of Beauty itself—the eternal, unchanging, and perfect Form of Beauty (in Platonic terms). This is a direct contemplation of the divine and the ultimate source of all beauty and truth.

The Ultimate Goal: Immortality through Love

Plato suggests that love is fundamentally a desire for immortality—either through:

• *Physical reproduction* (producing children, ensuring continuity), or

• *Intellectual and spiritual creation* (contributing ideas, art, and knowledge that live beyond one's lifetime).

I.2 Aristotle: Love as Friendship *(Philia)*

In his *Nicomachean Ethics,* Aristotle presents a profound understanding of love through the concept of friendship *(philia).* He classifies friendship into three distinct categories: utility friendship, pleasure friendship, and virtuous friendship. Each type of friendship is defined by its motivation and purpose, shaping the way individuals relate to one another.

Utility Friendship

Utility friendships are based on mutual benefits. These relationships exist primarily for practical reasons, where individuals engage with each other to gain something advantageous. Examples include business partnerships, political alliances, or even casual acquaintances who provide convenience. Such friendships are often short-lived, lasting only as long as the benefits continue to exist. Once the utility is no longer present, the bond dissolves. Aristotle sees this type of friendship as the least meaningful since it is based on external factors rather than genuine care for the other person.

Pleasure Friendship

Pleasure friendships arise from shared enjoyment, often rooted in physical attraction, entertainment, or common interests. These friendships are formed when individuals derive happiness from one another's company, such as friendships among young people who bond over similar hobbies or passions. Like utility friendships, these are often temporary and dependent on the fleeting nature of pleasure. When the enjoyment fades, the connection weakens. While these friendships can be meaningful in certain phases of life, Aristotle considers them inferior to those founded on virtue.

Virtuous Friendship

The highest and most enduring form of friendship, according

to Aristotle, is virtuous friendship. This type of friendship is based on mutual respect, admiration, and a sincere desire for the well-being and moral development of the other person. In virtuous friendships, individuals love each other for who they truly are, rather than for what they can gain. Such relationships require time, effort, and shared values. They contribute to personal growth and flourishing *(eudaimonia),* as they are built on trust, honesty, and a commitment to each other's character.

Aristotle views love as an ethical and communal bond that plays a crucial role in human flourishing. Unlike the other two types of friendship, virtuous friendships are rare but invaluable. They help individuals cultivate virtues such as kindness, generosity, and wisdom. In this way, Aristotle sees *philia* not just as an emotional connection but as a moral and philosophical ideal—one that allows people to become the best versions of themselves through meaningful relationships.

I.3 Christian and *Agape* Love (Unconditional Love)

Christian philosophy, particularly through the works of theologians like Augustine (d. 430) and Aquinas (d. 1274), introduces the concept of *agape*—a form of selfless, unconditional love. Unlike other forms of love that may be based on emotions, personal benefit, or attraction, agape transcends these limitations and is deeply rooted in the will and moral commitment to love others regardless of circumstances.

The Nature of *Agape* Love

Agape love is often associated with divine love, reflecting the boundless and sacrificial love of God for humanity. This love is not dependent on merit or reciprocation but is freely given. It is the type of love exemplified in Christian teachings, where believers are encouraged to love their neighbours, their enemies, and even those who wrong them.

I.3.1 Augustine and *Agape*

Augustine of Hippo emphasises that true love originates from God and is directed towards the ultimate good. He argues that human love should be oriented toward God and others rather than selfish desires. Augustine sees *agape* as a love that transforms the soul, drawing people closer to divine perfection and away from earthly temptations.

I.3.2 Aquinas and the Wilful Nature of *Agape*

Thomas Aquinas further develops the idea of *agape* by integrating it into his concept of charity, which he considers the highest form of love. According to Aquinas, *agape* is an act of the will rather than mere emotion. It involves choosing to love, to seek the good of others, and to act selflessly in a way that mirrors divine love. Aquinas links *agape* to the theological virtue of charity, which leads believers toward salvation and a harmonious relationship with God.

Agape in Christian Ethics

Agape love plays a fundamental role in Christian ethics and moral philosophy. It serves as the foundation for principles such as forgiveness, compassion, and altruism. The New Testament, particularly in the teachings of Jesus, repeatedly emphasises agape love as the highest commandment—*"Love your neighbor as yourself"* and *"Love one another as I have loved you."*

This kind of love is often expressed in acts of service, sacrifice, and compassion, as seen in the life of Jesus Christ. It inspires believers to put others before themselves, showing kindness even when it is undeserved.

Agape and Human Flourishing

While *agape* is deeply connected to Christian theology, its principles extend beyond religious belief and into broader discussions of ethics and human relationships. *Agape* love promotes a vision of humanity where people act with genuine concern for others, fostering social harmony and personal fulfilment. It is considered a love that cultivates both individual and communal well-being, as it encourages acts of generosity, understanding, and reconciliation.

Chapter II: Love in Modern Western philosophy

The concept of love in modern Western philosophy has been explored in various ways, often reflecting broader philosophical concerns about existence, morality, and the self. Love is discussed in relation to emotions, ethics, metaphysics, existentialism, and even political philosophy.

II.1 Rationalism & Enlightenment (17th–18th Century)

During the Enlightenment, love was often analysed through reason and human nature.

II.1.1 Love by René Descartes (d. 1650)

René Descartes, the 17th-century French philosopher and mathematician, did not write extensively on love in the way that he explored doubt, reason, and metaphysics. However, his work on emotions (or "passions"), particularly in *Les Passions de l'Âme (The Passions of the Soul, 1649),* provides insight into his understanding of love from a rationalist perspective.

Descartes' View on Love: A Rationalist Approach

Descartes saw love as one of the fundamental human emotions, classifying it as a passion of the soul that arises from perceptions of good or benefit. For him, love was not merely a sentimental or romantic feeling but an intellectual response tied to one's understanding of what is beneficial or desirable.

Definition of Love

Descartes defined love as *"a passion that incites the soul to join itself willingly to objects that appear suitable to it."* In other words, love is the emotional response that leads individuals to seek union with things they perceive as good or desirable.

Two Types of Love Descartes distinguished between two main types of love:

Intellectual (or Rational) Love: This is a form of love guided by reason and understanding, where one loves something for its inherent goodness and alignment with virtue.

Sensory (or Passionate) Love: This is driven by external influences, bodily sensations, and immediate pleasures rather than rational considerations.

Love and the Mind-Body Dualism

Descartes' dualism, which separates the mind from the body, plays a role in his understanding of love. While love is felt as an emotional passion (tied to bodily reactions like increased heart rate), he emphasised that the true essence of love exists in the soul, beyond mere physical attraction.

The Role of Will in Love

Since Descartes believed that reason and willpower govern human actions, he suggested that individuals can regulate and refine their love through intellectual effort. Unlike thinkers who saw love as uncontrollable, Descartes argued that one could direct love toward virtuous or beneficial ends through rational reflection.

Love, Joy, and Virtue

Descartes associated love with joy when it is directed toward good things and aligned with virtue. He also believed that love has the potential to strengthen human connections and moral behaviour when it is guided by reason rather than blind passion.

II.1.2 Love by Baruch Spinoza (d. 1677)

Baruch Spinoza, the 17th-century Dutch philosopher, approached love from a rational and metaphysical perspective, deeply rooted in his philosophical system of monism, determinism, and ethical rationalism. His concept of love is closely tied to his understanding of God, nature, and human emotions, as presented in his magnum opus, *Ethics*.

Love as an Emotion and Its Nature

In *Ethics,* Spinoza defines love as:

"Love is pleasure accompanied by the idea of an external cause." (Ethics, Part III, Proposition 13, Scholium)

This means that love arises when we experience joy and attribute that joy to an external cause. Love, like all emotions in Spinoza's philosophy, is determined by the fundamental laws of nature and follows from the way we perceive and understand the world.

Spinoza categorises emotions into passive and active affects:

Passive love: When love is driven by external causes, such as physical attraction or transient pleasures, it remains a passive emotion that can enslave us.

Active love: When love is guided by reason and understanding, it becomes an empowering force that leads to greater joy and freedom.

Love and Understanding:

One of Spinoza's most famous ideas is the intellectual love of God, which is the highest form of love. He argues that since God (or Nature) is the ultimate reality, true love arises from an intellectual understanding of this reality.

This love is:

Rational: Unlike emotional attachment to fleeting things, the intellectual love of God is based on an understanding of the unity of all things.

Liberating: It frees individuals from suffering, fear, and the bondage of passions.

Eternal: Since it is based on knowledge of the eternal nature of reality, it is not subject to decay like personal or material attachments.

Love and Freedom

For Spinoza, freedom is not the absence of necessity but the understanding of necessity. In love, this means:

True love is based on knowledge: If we love something blindly, we are at the mercy of external forces, but if we love based on an understanding of its nature, our love becomes an expression of our rational freedom.

Love without possession: Because everything follows from the necessity of nature, love is not about controlling or owning another person but about recognising their essence and role in the grand scheme of existence

Love as the highest virtue: Spinoza sees love as an essential aspect of human flourishing *(conatus*—the striving for self-preservation). Through love grounded in reason, we align ourselves with the fundamental drive of nature.

Love and Ethics

Spinoza's ethical system is based on achieving joy through understanding. He believes that:

Love can lead to greater perfection: If love is grounded in reason and directed toward what is eternal and necessary, it leads to greater contentment and enlightenment.

Hatred is overcome by love: He famously states that *"hatred can never be good,"* and that the best way to combat negative emotions is through an active, rational love of what is truly good.

II.1.3 Love by Immanuel Kant (d. 1804)

Immanuel Kant proposed a moral framework rooted in duty and rationality rather than emotional inclination. His ethical system, deontological ethics, asserts that moral actions are determined by duty rather than personal desires or inclinations. This perspective extends to love, which Kant saw not merely as an emotion but as a moral obligation.

Love Beyond Emotion

Kant distinguished between two forms of love: pathological love and practical love. Pathological love refers to emotional or sentimental affection, which is fleeting and subject to personal inclinations. Practical love, on the other hand, is a form of ethical duty—it is love guided by moral principles and reason, rather than by transient feelings.

He believed that true love is demonstrated through ethical actions and a commitment to treating others with respect and dignity. This means that even in the absence of warm feelings, individuals have a duty to act lovingly toward one another. For example, helping a stranger, showing kindness to an adversary, or fulfilling familial responsibilities despite personal resentment are expressions of moral love.

Love as a Moral Duty

For Kant, moral love aligns with his categorical imperative, which dictates that we should act according to maxims that we would will to become universal laws. This means that love, as a duty, should be performed universally and not be dependent on personal emotions or inclinations. The fundamental principle is that every human being possesses intrinsic worth, and our moral duty is to respect and uphold this worth through ethical actions.

One key formulation of the categorical imperative states that we should treat others as ends in themselves, never merely as means to an end. In the context of love, this implies that genuine love is not about personal gain or pleasure but about moral commitment to the well-being of others. Love, in this sense, becomes a rational and ethical duty rather than an emotion that fluctuates with time and circumstance.

Practical Implications of Kantian Love

Marital and Familial Love – According to Kant, love in marriage should not be driven solely by passion, which may fade, but by mutual respect and ethical commitment. Similarly, parental love is not merely a natural instinct but also a moral duty to care for and educate children.

Love in Society – Moral love extends to how we treat our neighbors, coworkers, and even strangers. It demands fairness, kindness, and respect in all human interactions, ensuring that we act justly regardless of our personal feelings.

Love and Charity – Acts of charity and altruism should not stem only from sentimental pity but from a sense of moral duty to help those in need. True generosity, in the Kantian sense, arises from the recognition of others' humanity and the obligation to support them.

II.2 Romanticism & Idealism (19th Century)

This period saw a shift toward the emotional and metaphysical aspects of love.

II.2.1 Love by G.W.F. Hegel (d. 1831)

G.W.F. Hegel's concept of love is deeply tied to his broader philosophical system, particularly his ideas on dialectics, recognition, and unity-in-difference. While he does not provide a single, systematic account of love, his discussions of it appear in works such as Phenomenology of Spirit, Elements of the Philosophy of Right, and his lectures on ethics and religion.

Hegel's Definition of Love

Hegel views love as a dialectical unity of individuals—one that transcends the isolation of individual selfhood while maintaining differentiation. He describes love as a process in which the self negates its isolated subjectivity and finds itself again in the unity of the relationship.

Love as a Unity of Difference

Love involves a contradiction: individuals give up their self-centered independence but, in doing so, actually realize a deeper form of selfhood.

He writes: *"Love means in general the consciousness of my unity with another, so that I am not isolated in my individuality, but gain my self-consciousness only through renouncing my independent existence and knowing myself as the unity of myself with another and of the other with me."*

Love and the Dialectic of Recognition

In *Phenomenology of Spirit,* Hegel explores the idea that human identity is formed through recognition by others.

Love is a higher form of recognition, where two individuals mutually affirm each other without domination or negation.

Unlike in the *Master-Slave Dialectic,* where recognition is asymmetric and results in struggle, love is a free and equal recognition.

Love and Ethical Life *(Sittlichkeit)*

Love is foundational to the ethical life, especially in the family.

In *Philosophy of Right,* he sees marriage as an ethical institution where individuals transcend self-interest and form a unified whole.

Love in the family serves as a natural form of ethical unity, though it must be complemented by rational institutions (such as the state) to achieve full freedom.

Love and Religion

Hegel sees Christian love *(agape)* as an expression of divine unity, where individuals are reconciled in absolute spirit.

Religious love mirrors philosophical love, in that both involve self-transcendence and unity in a higher whole.

II.2.2 Love by Arthur Schopenhauer (d. 1860)

Arthur Schopenhauer, one of the most influential pessimistic philosophers of the 19th century, viewed love not as a divine or romantic ideal but as a biological mechanism engineered by nature to perpetuate life. In his work *The World as Will and Representation,* Schopenhauer presents love as a manifestation of the "will to life", an unconscious and primal force that governs all living beings. According to him, our romantic inclinations, desires, and emotional attachments are mere illusions created by this will, designed not for personal happiness but for the reproduction and preservation of the species.

Love as a Deception of the Individual

Schopenhauer argued that individuals mistakenly believe they fall in love out of personal preference, shared interests, or emotional compatibility. In reality, he contended, the choices we make in selecting partners are dictated by an instinctive drive to produce the healthiest offspring. Our attraction to particular traits—

such as facial symmetry, physical strength, or reproductive vitality—stems not from aesthetic preference but from an unconscious calculation of genetic fitness. Even the emotional turmoil, passion, and heartbreak associated with love serve the greater purpose of compelling individuals to engage in relationships that, in turn, contribute to the survival of the species.

This perspective turns the conventional understanding of love on its head. Rather than being a source of fulfilment and meaning, love, for Schopenhauer, is a cruel trick played by nature. The individual is merely a pawn in a larger biological game, pursuing desires that serve an impersonal and indifferent force. Love is not meant to bring happiness to the lover but to guarantee the continuation of life—once reproduction has occurred, the passion that once burned so intensely often fades, revealing the transient and illusory nature of romantic love.

The Tragedy of Love

Schopenhauer's analysis of love leads to a bleak conclusion: love is inherently linked to suffering. He noted that the strongest romantic passions often lead to the greatest miseries, whether through unfulfilled longing, jealousy, or the inevitable dissatisfaction that follows romantic success. Moreover, love frequently forces individuals into life choices they might otherwise avoid, such as unhappy marriages or sacrifices made in the name of an idealised union. In this sense, love is not a blessing but a form of bondage, where individuals are manipulated by the will to life without their conscious awareness.

This perspective aligns with Schopenhauer's broader pessimism about human existence. He believed life itself is characterised by endless striving and suffering, and love is merely one more way in which the will deceives us into participating in this endless cycle. The promise of fulfilment through romantic love is, for him, one of the greatest illusions of all.

Influence and Modern Interpretations

Schopenhauer's view of love as a biological illusion anticipated later developments in psychology and evolutionary biology. Thinkers like Sigmund Freud and modern evolutionary theorists have echoed his claim that human attraction is largely driven by subconscious instincts aimed at reproduction. Contemporary discussions on mate selection, genetic compatibility, and evolutionary psychology often reflect his insights, even if they do not share his explicitly pessimistic outlook.

Despite its bleakness, Schopenhauer's theory provides a compelling explanation for many of love's paradoxes. It sheds light on why people often fall for partners who may not be compatible in the long run and why the most intense romantic experiences can be accompanied by profound suffering. While modern society tends to romanticise love, Schopenhauer's philosophy serves as a sobering reminder that much of what we cherish in romantic relationships may be nothing more than nature's grand deception.

II.2.3 Love by Friedrich Nietzsche (d. 1900)

Friedrich Nietzsche's philosophy of love is complex and often unconventional. Unlike the romantic or idealistic perspectives on love, Nietzsche viewed it through the lens of power, self-overcoming, and human nature.

Love as a Will to Power

Nietzsche saw love as an expression of the Will to Power—the fundamental drive in all life to assert itself, grow, and overcome. Love, in his view, is not purely selfless but is often intertwined with the desire to possess, control, or elevate the self.

"Ultimately, it is the desire, not the desired, that we love." (The Gay Science)

This suggests that love is often more about our inner longing than about the object of affection itself.

Beyond Romantic Idealism

Nietzsche was skeptical of idealised, self-sacrificing love, particularly as it was presented in Christian and moral traditions. He criticised how love was often linked with self-denial and duty rather than an affirmation of life.

"The love of one is a barbarism: for it is exercised at the expense of all others. The love of God also." (Beyond Good and Evil)

Here, he points out how exclusive love, whether for a person or a deity, can limit and suppress broader experiences of life.

The Danger of Possessive Love

Nietzsche warned against love that seeks to dominate or enslave the beloved. He saw possessive love as a weakness, where one person tries to complete themselves through another rather than affirm their own strength.

"In women, love is an activity, not a passive state; it is an aggressive approach, the most ardent pursuit of conquest." (Beyond Good and Evil)

He believed that love, particularly when mixed with insecurity, often turns into a will to dominate rather than a mutual experience of growth.

Love as Self-Overcoming

For Nietzsche, the highest form of love aligns with self-overcoming—where love inspires both individuals to grow beyond themselves. He admired passionate, life-affirming love that did not weaken but rather strengthened individuals.

"What is done out of love always takes place beyond good and evil." (Beyond Good and Evil)

This means true love should not be constrained by moral expectations or societal norms, but rather serve as a means for personal evolution.

Amor Fati—Love for Life Itself

Nietzsche's ultimate notion of love may be amor fati—a deep, unconditional love for life in its entirety, including suffering and imperfection.

"My formula for greatness in a human being is amor fati: that one wants nothing to be different, not forward, not backward, not in all eternity." (Ecce Homo)

Rather than seeking completeness in another person, Nietzsche urges us to embrace all of life—its struggles, pain, and joys—with love.

II.3 Existentialism & Phenomenology (20th Century)

Love was deeply explored in relation to human freedom, existence, and relationships.

Existentialist thinkers like Jean-Paul Sartre and Simone de Beauvoir redefine love in terms of freedom and responsibility, moving away from traditional notions of possession, dependency, and romantic idealisation. They argue that love should not be about control or the subjugation of one's identity to another but should instead be rooted in mutual recognition and respect for the other's autonomy.

II.3.1 Love by Jean-Paul Sartre (d. 1980)

Jean-Paul Sartre had a unique and often unsettling view on love. His perspective is deeply rooted in his broader existentialist ideas about freedom, human relationships, and self-deception.

Sartre on Love: A Conflict of Freedoms

Sartre saw love as a fundamentally paradoxical and conflict-ridden experience. He argued that love is a struggle for possession and recognition, but because humans are inherently free beings, this struggle is doomed to failure.

The Desire to Possess the Other

Sartre believed that when we love someone, we want them to love us in return, but not just as a casual emotion. We want them to freely choose us while at the same time wanting to control and possess their love.

The problem? True love requires the other person to willingly love us, but if we seek to control or secure that love, we rob them of their freedom.

The Look *("Le Regard")* and Objectification

Sartre introduced the concept of "the look" (le regard), where being seen by another person makes us aware of ourselves as an object in their world.

In love, this means we become vulnerable: we want the other person to see us as valuable, special, and unique. But as soon as they do, we may feel trapped by their perception of us.

Similarly, when we love someone, we often try to define or "fix" their identity, limiting their freedom.

Love as Bad Faith *(Mauvaise Foi)*

Sartre's idea of bad faith refers to self-deception, where we deny our own freedom or responsibility.

In love, people often fall into bad faith by either:

Becoming dependent on the other (losing themselves in the relationship)

Trying to dominate the other (controlling or defining their partner)

Either way, love often fails because one or both people struggle to maintain their freedom while wanting security in the relationship.

Love as an Impossible Project

Sartre ultimately sees love as a doomed project. Because humans are free and ever-changing, no love can remain stable without falling into bad faith. Love, in his view, is often a battle between two freedoms: one person trying to keep the other's love while maintaining their own independence.

This contrasts sharply with more romantic or idealistic views of love, which see it as harmonious or fulfilling. Sartre's perspective is rather pessimistic: love can never truly satisfy us because we desire something contradictory—both freedom and security at the same time.

Sartre's Love in Literature

In *No Exit,* one character famously says, *"Hell is other people"* (*L'enfer, c'est les autres*). This reflects how relationships, including love, often involve struggle, objectification, and conflict rather than pure happiness.

In *Nausea,* the protagonist struggles with relationships because he sees existence itself as absurd and meaningless, making love seem just as unstable.

II.3.2 Love by Simone de Beauvoir (d. 1986)

Simone de Beauvoir's concept of love, as explored in *The Second Sex* (1949) and other writings, is deeply intertwined with her existentialist and feminist philosophy. She critiques traditional notions of romantic love, particularly the ways in which they have historically subordinated women, and proposes a more authentic and reciprocal form of love based on mutual freedom and recognition.

Love and Existentialism

De Beauvoir, influenced by Jean-Paul Sartre's existentialist philosophy, argues that love should not be about possession or dependency but about freedom. Love, in her view, should not mean the loss of self but should instead be a relationship in which both partners remain autonomous individuals. She rejects the idea of romantic love as an absolute or a "destiny" for women, which she sees as a cultural construct designed to keep women subordinate.

Critique of Traditional Love

In *The Second Sex,* de Beauvoir examines how society conditions women to find their identity in love. She argues that in patriarchal cultures, women are often taught to define themselves in relation to men, making love the center of their existence. This leads to relationships where women sacrifice their freedom and individuality, becoming the "Other" in relation to the man, who is seen as the essential subject.

Authentic Love vs. Inauthentic Love

De Beauvoir distinguishes between authentic love, which is based on mutual respect an equality, and inauthentic love, where one partner dominates the other. She sees the traditional model of love as an asymmetrical power dynamic that often results in women's oppression. In contrast, authentic love allows both partners to exist as independent beings who choose to be together freely, rather than out of social obligation or existential need.

Love as a Creative Project

Rather than seeing love as a fixed, idealised state, de Beauvoir envisions it as an ongoing project—something that must be continually renewed through shared experiences, intellectual engagement, and personal growth. Love, in this sense, is not a passive surrender but an active and dynamic process that enhances the freedom of both individuals.

The Role of Friendship in Love

De Beauvoir also explores the idea that the best kind of love resembles deep friendship. She believed that true love should involve companionship, intellectual equality, and emotional support. Her lifelong relationship with Sartre reflected this vision, as they maintained an unconventional but deeply intellectual and emotionally significant bond.

Implications for Feminism

Her philosophy of love has had profound implications for feminist thought, particularly in critiquing the social expectation that women must find fulfilment solely through romantic relationships. She argues that women should seek personal and professional fulfilment independently of their relationships and that love should complement, not define, their existence.

II.3.3 Love by Emmanuel Levinas (d. 1995)

Emmanuel Levinas, a 20th-century French philosopher, developed a unique perspective on love rooted in his ethics of alterity (otherness). His approach to love is not centred on emotions, romance, or desire, as in traditional philosophical or literary conceptions. Instead, love, for Levinas, is deeply connected to the ethical relationship with the Other.

Love as an Ethical Encounter

For Levinas, love is fundamentally an ethical experience rather than a mere feeling. It arises from the face-to-face encounter with another person, where the Other's vulnerability and infinite alterity (difference) call us to responsibility. Love is not about possession or fusion, as in many traditional Western philosophical and literary conceptions, but about recognising and responding to the irreducible uniqueness of the Other.

Love and Responsibility

Levinas argues that love places an ethical demand upon us. When we encounter another person, particularly in their suffering or need, we are called to respond. This is not an obligation imposed by law or reason, but an intrinsic responsibility that arises from the encounter itself. Love, in this sense, is a movement beyond the self toward the Other, an openness that prioritizes their needs and well-being.

Love Beyond Reciprocity

Unlike many conceptions of love that involve mutual exchange (such as contractual or reciprocal love), Levinas' love does not require the Other to return the affection or ethical commitment. It is a form of generosity, a giving without expecting something in return. This makes love asymmetrical—it is not based on equality or mutual benefit, but on an unconditional ethical relation.

Love and the Face of the Other

The "face" plays a crucial role in Levinas' philosophy. It is not just the physical face of another person, but the presence of the Other that commands ethical responsibility. Love, then, is responding to the call of the face, an openness to the Other's needs that transcends self-interest.

Love and Infinity

In *Totality and Infinity,* Levinas contrasts totality (which absorbs the Other into the same) with infinity (which preserves the Other's alterity). Love, in its ethical sense, belongs to the realm of infinity because it does not seek to reduce the Other to an object or an extension of oneself. Instead, love respects and preserves the infinite distance and mystery of the Other.

Love and Filiation

In *Otherwise than Being,* Levinas extends his idea of love to the concept of "filiation" (parent-child relationships). He sees love in its purest form in the relationship between a parent and child, where the parent is entirely responsible for the child's well-being without expectation of return. This highlights love as an ethical obligation that extends into the future, beyond one's own existence.

Love as Transcendence

Levinas describes love as a force that transcends being. It is not about possessing the Other or merging with them, but about an ethical openness that allows for true alterity to exist. Love is thus a way of stepping beyond oneself, of being for the Other without reducing them to an object of desire or utility.

In practice, existentialist love demands an ongoing effort to balance intimacy with independence. It resists possessiveness and demands honesty, as true love cannot thrive on illusions or self-deception. Each lover must confront the challenge of affirming the other's freedom while maintaining their own, recognising that love is not about merging into a single entity but about two individuals who, in their freedom, choose to be together.

Ultimately, existentialist love is radical in its insistence that love should enhance rather than limit one's existence. It is a love that does not seek to escape the anxieties of freedom but embraces them, acknowledging that love, like life itself, is an act of constant becoming.

II.3.4 Love by Heidegger (d. 1976)

The idea of love in Heidegger's philosophy is not addressed in the same direct or sentimental way as in traditional philosophical or poetic treatments. However, by carefully interpreting his key concepts—especially from *Being and Time* (1927)—we can uncover a deep and unique understanding of love grounded in his existential ontology.

Being-with *(Mitsein):* Love as a mode of existence

For Heidegger, human beings *(Dasein)* are fundamentally being-with others. We are never isolated; our existence is always already in a shared world. Love, then, could be understood as an authentic mode of being-with another—a way of truly acknowledging, caring for, and existing alongside someone without reducing them to a mere object or role.

Love, in this sense, would not be possession or desire but a shared openness to Being itself through the presence of the other. It's an ontological relationship, not just an emotional or psychological state.

Care *(Sorge):* Love as care and solicitude

Heidegger describes care *(Sorge)* as the fundamental structure of Dasein. All of our projects, relationships, and concerns are expressions of care. Love, in Heideggerian terms, might be seen as an elevated form of care—what he calls solicitude *(Fürsorge),* the way we engage with others not as tools for our use but as beings whose own being matters.

Authentic love would involve freeing the other to be themselves, allowing them to fulfil their own potential without domination. Inauthentic love, by contrast, might seek to control, manipulate, or subsume the other into one's own plans.

Authenticity *(Eigentlichkeit):* Love as the shared facing of finitude

A crucial part of Heidegger's philosophy is the confrontation with Being-towards-death. Authenticity arises when we accept our own mortality and live with an awareness of the finitude of

In love, authenticity might mean facing mortality together—acknowledging that our time together is limited and therefore infinitely precious. This doesn't lead to despair but to a deeper appreciation of the other as a unique and finite being.

Love, then, could be seen as a shared being-towards-death, where two people support each other in the existential task of living meaningfully in the face of their shared finitude.

Letting-be *(Gelassenheit):* Love as letting the other be

Later in his career, Heidegger emphasised *Gelassenheit,* or releasement. This is the idea of allowing things (and people) to be as they are without forcing them into our frameworks.

In love, this would mean not imposing our own desires or expectations on the beloved but letting them unfold in their own way. It's a love that gives space rather than grasps—a kind of patient, open attentiveness.

II.3.5 Love by Kierkegaard (d. 1855)

Kierkegaard's concept of love is deeply philosophical, existential, and rooted in his Christian worldview. He develops the idea of love most extensively in his work *"Works of Love"* (1847), where he reflects on what it truly means to love, beyond romantic or preferential attachments.

Love as a Duty, Not a Feeling

For Kierkegaard, love is not primarily about emotions or passion. Those are fleeting and unreliable. Instead, love is an obligation—a command from God. Specifically, he references the Biblical commandment:

"You shall love your neighbour as yourself."

This means that love isn't based on whether someone is lovable, interesting, or attractive. True love exists even when feelings fade because it's grounded in duty and commitment.

Neighbour-Love *(Agape)*

Kierkegaard emphasises neighbour-love, which differs from:

Eros (romantic love)

Philia (friendship)

Neighbour-love is unconditional, universal, and eternal. Everyone is your neighbour, including people you dislike or don't know. Love of neighbour transcends preferences, social distinctions, and personal desires.

This form of love is selfless and sacrificial. It's about willing the good of the other, regardless of what you get in return.

The Infinite vs. The Finite in Love

Human love (like romantic or friendship love) often begins as preferential and finite—based on specific qualities we admire. But Kierkegaard pushes us toward infinite love, which is grounded in the eternal, unchanging love of God.

Finite love Subject to change and decay.

Infinite love → Rooted in the divine, which sustains love even through hardship, boredom, or loss.

Love Builds Up

One of Kierkegaard's key ideas is that love builds up. When you truly love someone, you are not trying to possess them or control them. Instead, your love helps them grow and flourish as individuals.

True love isn't about taking; it's about giving without expectation. It's active, creative, and transformative.

Self-Love and Love of Others

Kierkegaard also explores the tension between self-love and loving others. The command to *"love your neighbour as yourself"* implies that healthy self-love is necessary. If you despise yourself, your love for others will be distorted. But if you love yourself rightly—seeing yourself as created and loved by God—then you can love others properly.

Love as the fulfilment of Faith

For Kierkegaard, love and faith are inseparable. Faith in God manifests through the way we love others. Without love, faith becomes empty or hypocritical. To truly live as a Christian is to love endlessly and sacrificially.

II.4 Psychoanalytic and Structuralist Influences

The concept of love is understood through Psychoanalytic and Structuralist lenses. These two schools of thought come from different angles—psychoanalysis delves into the unconscious, while structuralism looks at the deep structures of language and culture—but both provide rich interpretations of human experience, including love.

II.4.1 Love by Sigmund Freud (d. 1939)

Sigmund Freud, the father of psychoanalysis, developed a complex and multi-faceted understanding of love, deeply rooted in his theories of the unconscious, sexuality, and human development. Freud saw love as an expression of psychic energy, primarily stemming from the libido, which is the driving force behind all human behaviour. His concept of love is closely tied to his broader theories on sexuality, attachment, and psychological development.

Love as a Manifestation of *Libido*

Freud believed that love originates from the *libido,* or sexual energy, which drives human relationships. He argued that all forms of love—whether romantic, platonic, or familial—are based on the redirection and sublimation of this sexual energy. This means that love is fundamentally linked to our desires and instincts, even when it appears non-sexual.

Stages of Love Development

Freud connected love to his psychosexual stages of development:

Oral Stage (0-1 year): The first experience of love is between the infant and the mother, where love is intertwined with nourishment and dependency.

Anal Stage (1-3 years): The child begins to develop autonomy and control, influencing future expressions of love through power and order.

Phallic Stage (3-6 years): The *Oedipus Complex* emerges, where the child experiences a deep attachment to the opposite-sex parent and rivalry with the same-sex parent, shaping future romantic preferences.

Latency Stage (6-12 years): Sexual impulses are repressed, and children focus on friendships and social bonds.

Genital Stage (12+ years): Mature love develops, directed towards partners outside the family, integrating emotional and sexual intimacy.

The *Oedipus Complex* and Love

Freud's most controversial theory, the *Oedipus Complex,* suggests that a child's early attachment to the opposite-sex parent plays a foundational role in their later love relationships. He argued that unresolved childhood conflicts could manifest in adult romantic choices and patterns, often leading individuals to seek partners resembling their parents.

Types of Love

Freud distinguished between different kinds of love:

Sensual (Eros) Love: Love that is rooted in sexual desire, passion, and physical attraction.

Tender (Affectionate) Love: More connected to deep emotional bonds, care, and long-term attachment.

Narcissistic Love: Self-love or love directed towards an idealised version of oneself in another person.

Sublimated Love: When sexual energy is redirected into non-sexual pursuits, such as creative work, philanthropy, or intellectual endeavours.

Love and Repetition Compulsion

Freud believed that people tend to repeat relationship patterns from childhood, even when they are unhealthy. This concept, known as repetition compulsion, explains why individuals might unconsciously seek partners who resemble their early caregivers or repeat past traumas in love relationships.

Love as an Illusion

Freud was often skeptical about the idealised notions of romantic love. He saw love as a mix of biological drives, childhood conditioning, and unconscious desires rather than as a purely spiritual or emotional connection. He believed that much of love is driven by unconscious motives, such as the need to resolve past conflicts or fulfil unfulfilled desires.

II.4.2 Love by Jacques Lacan (d. 1981)

Jacques Lacan, a prominent French psychoanalyst, offered a nuanced perspective on love, intertwining it with his theories of desire, lack, and the structures of human psychology.

Love as Recognition of Lack

Central to Lacan's theory is the idea that love involves acknowledging and representing the other's lack. He posited that in love, individuals give what they do not possess, symbolising their own fundamental absence or incompleteness. This act of giving highlights the mutual recognition of each other's deficiencies, forming the basis of a profound connection. Lacan articulated this in his Seminar X, stating:

"What we give in love is essentially what we do not have."

Narcissism and the Imaginary Order

Lacan expanded on Freud's concept of narcissism, suggesting that love often emerges from self-love. In the "Imaginary" order, individuals fall in love with an image or ideal ego that reflects their own aspirations for wholeness. This projection means that the beloved embodies traits the lover desires for themselves, leading to a form of love that is, at its core, self-referential. As Renata Salecl describes:

"We love this person because of the perfection we have striven to reach for our own ego."

The Role of the Symbolic and the Other

Beyond the Imaginary, Lacan emphasised the "Symbolic" order, where language and societal structures reside. In this realm, love is intertwined with desire and the "Other." He famously stated:

"Man's desire is the desire of the Other."

This suggests that our desires are shaped by the desires of others, and in love, we seek recognition and validation from the Other, striving to be the object of their desire.

Sublimation and the Quest for the Lost Object

Lacan also discussed the concept of *"Das Ding" (the Thing)*, representing an unattainable object of desire. In love, individuals often sublimate, redirecting their desires toward a person or object that symbolises this elusive "Thing." This process involves elevating the loved one to a status that fills the void left by the unattainable object, though this fulfilment is always temporary and incomplete. Michel Foucault (1926–1984) examined love in terms of power relations, especially in The History of Sexuality, arguing that love is historically constructed through discourses of sexuality.

II.4.3 Love by Robert Sternberg (1949-)

Robert Sternberg, a psychologist known for his *Triangular Theory of Love,* proposed that love consists of three key components:

Intimacy – Emotional closeness, bonding, and connection in a relationship.

Passion – Physical attraction, romantic feelings, and sexual desire.

Commitment – The decision to stay in love and maintain a long-term relationship.

Developing Love Based on Sternberg's Theory:

To build a strong and lasting love, you can focus on enhancing all three components:

Building Intimacy (Emotional Connection)

Spend quality time together.

Engage in deep and meaningful conversations.

Show empathy, listen actively, and validate feelings.

Share personal experiences, dreams, and fears to build trust.

Express appreciation and gratitude regularly.

Strengthening Passion (Romantic & Physical Attraction)

Keep the spark alive through romantic gestures (dates, surprises, love notes).

Maintain physical affection (holding hands, hugs, kisses).

Engage in exciting activities together to keep the excitement alive.

Be open about desires and needs in the relationship.

Try new experiences to avoid routine and monotony.

Cultivating Commitment (Dedication & Loyalty)

Make conscious choices to prioritise the relationship.

Work through conflicts with patience and respect.

Stay honest and transparent with each other.

Support each other's personal growth and goals.

Build a shared vision for the future (e.g., marriage, family, or long-term goals).

Types of Love According to Sternberg

Depending on how these three components combine, different types of love emerge:

Liking/Friendship (Intimacy only)

Infatuation (Passion only)

Empty Love (Commitment only)

Romantic Love (Intimacy + Passion)

Companionate Love (Intimacy + Commitment)

Fatuous Love (Passion + Commitment)

Consummate Love (Intimacy + Passion + Commitment) → The ideal form of love

To develop Consummate Love, you need to actively nurture all three components over time.

II.4.4 Love by Luce Irigaray (1930-)

Luce Irigaray's concept of love is one of the most beautiful and complex parts of her philosophy. For her, love is deeply tied to her idea of "sexual difference", not just as a biological distinction but as a space of radical otherness and respectful relation. She's thinking beyond traditional, romantic, or even psychoanalytic notions of love and trying to imagine a love that preserves difference rather than erasing it.

Love as Recognition of the Other

For Irigaray, true love means recognising the other as irreducibly other. In much of Western thought and practice, relationships (especially between men and women) have been based on appropriation or assimilation—the other is either made the same or used as a mirror to reflect the self.

She critiques this dynamic, suggesting that genuine love can only occur when we allow the other to remain different, outside of our control or full understanding.

"To love is to recognise the irreducibility of the other, to keep open a space for the other's becoming."

Two-Subject Economy

Irigaray is famous for proposing that love has traditionally been organised around one subject (the male, historically), with the other (the female) functioning as object or support.

Her philosophy of love demands a "two-subject" relationship, where both partners exist as autonomous beings, and neither is reduced to a function of the other's desire.

Love, for her, becomes an ethical relation that requires ongoing negotiation and respect for each other's space, silence, and mystery.

Breath, Space, and Proximity

A beautiful metaphor she often uses for love is breath. For Irigaray, love is not about fusion (becoming one) but about being close while preserving air between us.

She talks about "between-ness"—the space that allows two people to exist together without suffocating or overwhelming each other.

It's a kind of tender distance

Close enough to touch.

Far enough to let the other breathe and grow.

Cultivating Love

Irigaray suggests love is not just a feeling, but a practice, something that must be cultivated like a garden.

She speaks of love as ethical work—learning how to listen to the other, to wait, to receive, to give without domination. This is why she often references Eastern philosophies like yoga and meditation, which teach attentiveness, patience, and respect for silence.

Love and Language

Since so much of Irigaray's work focuses on language, she also argues that part of loving is finding new ways of speaking—ways that don't dominate, categorise, or control the other.

This could mean:

Leaving space for silence.

Speaking poetically.

Using metaphors that evoke fluidity, multiplicity, and openness.

II.5 Contemporary Perspectives

A contemporary philosophical understanding of love, drawing from thinkers like Alain Badiou and Slavojiek, challenges both traditional romantic idealism and postmodern cynicism. Their perspectives emphasise love as an event that disrupts our habitual experience and restructures subjectivity.

II.5.1 Love by Alain Badiou (1931-)

Love as an Event of Truth

For Badiou, love is an event—a rupture in our existence that forces a reconfiguration of our worldview. Drawing from his broader ontology, love is one of the four truth procedures (alongside science, art, and politics). He argues that true love is not merely an attraction or an emotional experience but rather an engagement with difference that produces new truth.

• *Love and Subjectivity:* Love challenges the idea of a self-contained individual. Instead, it forces one to see the world from the perspective of the Two—an intersubjective transformation. This is a radical stance against consumerist and utilitarian approaches to love, which reduce relationships to personal gratification.

• *Love's Persistence:* Love, in Badiou's view, is not just the moment of falling in love but the work of sustaining love despite hardships. It is a continuous process of constructing a shared world.

II.5.2 Love by Slavoj Žižek (1949-)

Love, Ideology, and the Real

Žižek's perspective on love is heavily influenced by Lacanian psychoanalysis and ideological critique. He rejects the romantic notion of love as perfect harmony, instead seeing it as a traumatic encounter with the Real—the unassimilable core of the other.

• *Love as Loss and Disruption:* Žižek argues that love is not about finding a perfect match but about embracing imperfection. The idea that love completes us is an ideological fantasy; real love involves accepting the other in their radical alterity.

• *Love and Commodification:* In a capitalist world, love is commodified—dating apps, self-help books, and market-driven romance turn love into a consumer choice. True love, for Žižek, disrupts this logic, as it is fundamentally an irrational and excessive commitment.

• *The Ethics of Love:* Love is not about fusion but rather about maintaining a gap between oneself and the other while still remaining committed. It is an encounter that reveals how our desire is structured by the unconscious.

Love in Contemporary Society

Both Badiou and Žižek critique modern notions of love that prioritise self-interest, convenience, and compatibility over transformation and struggle. In an age of digital romance, where love is increasingly mediated by algorithms, their work challenges us to think of love as something more than an extension of neoliberal choice-making.

• Love as an ethical commitment rather than a fleeting passion.

• Love as a break from ideological constraints, revealing the subject's deeper structure.

• Love as an act of courage in a world that seeks to rationalise and control it.

II.5.3 Love by Martinus Thomsen (d. 1981)

Martinus' Idea of Love

Martinus Thomsen, a Danish spiritual philosopher and mystic, often just called Martinus developed a comprehensive spiritual cosmology, sometimes referred to as *Martinus Cosmology* or *The Third Testament*.

Martinus' philosophy revolves around universal love as the highest and ultimate principle of existence. His ideas about love are deeply spiritual, emphasising an evolutionary journey where humanity progresses toward a higher state of consciousness, characterised by selfless, all-encompassing love.

Love as the Core of the Universe

• Martinus believed that the entire universe is governed by love, and that all experiences (both joyful and painful) ultimately serve a divine purpose.

• He saw God as an all-loving being, with existence itself as an expression of divine love.

Personal vs. Universal Love

• Personal love (romantic or familial love) is part of human experience, but it is limited and often tied to ego-driven desires.

• Universal love (or "neighbourly love") is the highest form of love, extending beyond personal relationships to include all beings.

• True love, according to Martinus, is impartial, unconditional, and free of jealousy or possessiveness.

Love and Spiritual Evolution

• Martinus proposed that humanity is evolving spiritually toward a "real human kingdom," where love will no longer be exclusive but will embrace all life.

• He believed reincarnation plays a role in this process—each lifetime teaches us lessons about love, empathy, and understanding.

Suffering as a Path to Love

• According to Martinus, pain and suffering are not punishments but necessary experiences that refine our ability to love.

• Through suffering, we develop compassion, humility, and an understanding of others' pain.

This transformation leads to a state where we can love all beings.

The Role of Forgiveness

• A key aspect of love in Martinus' teachings is forgiveness. He saw it as a natural result of understanding that everyone is on their own evolutionary path.

• When we recognise that even those who harm us are simply at a different stage of development, we can forgive them out of love and wisdom.

Love as the Future of Humanity

• Martinus envisioned a future where wars, hatred, and selfishness would disappear as humanity awakens to the reality of universal love.

• He believed that humans would eventually become "Christ-beings," embodying the same all-encompassing love that Jesus demonstrated.

Chapter III: Love in Eastern Philosophy

The concept of love in Eastern philosophy is vast and multiface-ted, encompassing various dimensions such as compassion, devotion, selflessness, and interconnectedness. Unlike Western traditions that often emphasise romantic love, Eastern philosophy tends to focus on broader, more universal aspects of love.

III.1 Love in Hinduism

The concept of love in Hinduism is vast, multifaceted, and deeply embedded in its philosophy, mythology, and practice. Love is not merely an emotion but a profound spiritual force that connects beings to one another and to the divine.

Prema and Bhakti: Love as Devotion

Bhakti (devotional love) is one of the most celebrated forms of love in Hinduism, especially in the Bhakti movement, where love for the divine transcends all worldly attachments.

Saints like Mirabai (d. 1547), Ramanuja (d. 1137), and Tulasidas (d. 1623) expressed their intense love for gods such as Krishna and Rama through poetry, music, and spiritual practice.

Prema (pure love) is considered the highest form of love, where the devotee's love for God is unconditional and selfless, akin to the love of the *gopis* (cowherd women) for Krishna in the Bhagavata Purana.

Kama: Love as Desire

Kama, one of the four *Purusharthas* (goals of life), represents love in the form of desire, passion, and sensual pleasure.

The *Kama Sutra,* attributed to Vatsyayana, explores love, relationships, and aesthetics, highlighting that love in its physical form is a natural and vital aspect of human experience when pursued within *dharma* (righteousness).

Karuna: Love as Compassion

Karuna (compassionate love) is a form of universal love that encourages kindness and empathy towards all living beings.

This form of love is deeply rooted in the concept of *Ahimsa* (non-violence), as advocated by Mahatma Gandhi, and aligns with Hinduism's reverence for all forms of life.

Madhurya Bhava: Love as Sweetness

The *madhurya bhava* (sweet or romantic sentiment) between Radha and Krishna is one of the most iconic representations of divine love in Hinduism.

Their relationship symbolises the soul's longing and eventual union with the supreme consciousness, emphasising that true love transcends the material world.

Parental and Familial Love

Vatsalya (parental love) is exemplified in Hindu epics such as the *Ramayana and Mahabharata,* where relationships between parents and children, like King Dasharatha and Rama or Kunti and her sons, illustrate love as duty, sacrifice, and care.

Universal Love in *Advaita* Philosophy

In *Advaita Vedanta,* love is the recognition of the self in all beings. *Brahman* (the ultimate reality) is seen as the essence of all existence, and love emerges from the realisation that all is one.

Adi Shankaracharya taught that love, when stripped of ego and attachment, leads to liberation *(moksha).*

Love in Hindu Rituals and Festivals

Hindu festivals like Holi, which celebrates the playful love of Krishna and Radha, and Karva Chauth, which honours marital love, reflect how love permeates daily life and religious practice.

III.2 Love in Tantra

In Tantra, love is seen as a sacred and transformative force, a path to spiritual awakening and divine union. Unlike conventional views of love, Tantra perceives it as an energy that transcends mere emotions and physical attraction, leading to deeper states of consciousness and oneness with existence.

Cultivating Self-Love and Awareness

Before truly loving another, Tantra emphasises the importance of self-love. This means accepting yourself completely, including your desires, imperfections, and emotions. Meditation, self-inquiry, and breath-work help deepen awareness and bring balance to your inner energies.

Embracing Love as Divine Energy

In Tantra, love is not just a feeling but a sacred energy—*Shakti* (feminine energy) and *Shiva* (masculine consciousness). These two principles exist within everyone. Cultivating love means balancing these energies through practices like meditation, yoga, and mindful connection with yourself and your partner.

Conscious Connection with a Partner

Tantra teaches that true intimacy goes beyond physical connection.

To develop love in Tantra:

Practice deep eye gazing (soul gazing) to connect beyond the physical.

Engage in synchronised breathing to attune with each other's energy.

Listen with full presence, without judgment.

Slow down and be mindful in touch, presence, and communication.

Transforming Sexual Energy into Love

Tantric love is about harnessing sexual energy and using it to deepen connection rather than dissipating it quickly. This involves:

Viewing intimacy as a meditative and sacred act.

Extending pleasure through breath control and energy circulation.

Channeling sexual energy into heart-centred love.

Heart-Centred Meditation

Practices like the *Anahata* (heart chakra) meditation help open the heart to unconditional love. This can be done through:

Chanting the mantra *"Yam"* to activate the heart chakra.

Practicing *Metta* (loving-kindness) meditation to send love to yourself and others.

Visualising a golden light expanding from your heart, filling your body and surroundings.

Surrender and Trust

Love in Tantra is about letting go of ego, control, and fear. True love arises from surrendering to the flow of life and trusting in the divine intelligence guiding relationships. Practicing non-attachment while being fully present in love allows deeper emotional and spiritual intimacy.

Seeing the Divine in Your Partner

In Tantra, every being is seen as an expression of the divine. When you look at your partner, see them not just as a person but as an embodiment of love, wisdom, and the divine energy of the universe. This shifts love from possessiveness to reverence and deep connection.

Living Love Beyond Relationships

Tantric love is not limited to romantic relationships; it is a way of being. It means radiating love in all aspects of life—through compassion, presence, and connection with nature, people, and the universe.

III.3 Love in Buddhism

In Buddhism, love is developed through practices like *metta* (loving-kindness), *karuna* (compassion), *mudita* (sympathetic joy), and *upekkha* (equanimity)—known as the *Four Brahmaviharas* or the "Four Immeasurable."

Metta (Loving-kindness):

Mettma is unconditional, selfless love that seeks the happiness and well-being of all beings.

The *Metta Bhavana* meditation helps practitioners cultivate loving-kindness by starting with oneself and gradually extending love to others—loved ones, neutral people, difficult people, and finally all beings.

Metta encourages breaking down barriers of hatred, anger, and ill-will.

Karuna (Compassion):

Karuna is the deep wish for all beings to be free from suffering.

It involves empathy and active efforts to alleviate others' pain.

Compassion arises naturally when one recognises the shared experience of suffering in the cycle of *Samsara* (birth, death, and rebirth).

Mudita (Sympathetic Joy):

Mudita is the ability to feel joy in the happiness and success of others without jealousy or envy.

It fosters positive connections with others and diminishes self-centredness.

Upekkha (Equanimity):

Upekkha is balanced love—maintaining calmness and impartiality, even amidst life's ups and downs.

It ensures that love is steady and not swayed by personal attachment or aversion.

How to Develop Love in Buddhism:

Meditation practices: Metta Bhavana meditation is key, but mindfulness meditation also helps in understanding oneself and others.

Ethical living (Sila): Following the Five Precepts cultivates kindness in action.

Wisdom (Prajna): Insight into the nature of impermanence and interconnectedness enhances love and reduces attachment.

Daily acts of kindness: Practicing generosity *(Dana)* and patience (Khanti) fosters loving relationships.

Love vs. Attachment

Buddhism distinguishes between love *(metta)* and attachment *(tanha).* Love in Buddhism is selfless and freeing, while attachment leads to suffering due to clinging.

III.4 Love in Taoism

In Taoism, love is viewed through the lens of harmony, balance, and the interconnectedness of all things. Unlike more structured or romanticised notions of love found in Western philosophy, Taoist love is often subtle, flowing, and natural, much like the Tao itself—the fundamental principle that underlies and unites the universe.

Wu Wei (Effortless Action)

Taoist love is spontaneous and unforced, arising naturally without effort. True love, in this sense, is not something to be pursued aggressively but something that manifests when individuals are in harmony with themselves and the world around them.

In relationships, this translates to acceptance and allowing each person to grow and flow naturally, rather than imposing control or expectations.

Compassion and Kindness

Taoism emphasises compassion, one of the essential virtues along with humility and frugality. Compassionate love is seen as a fundamental part of living in accordance with the Tao.

Laozi, in the Tao Te Ching, highlights gentleness and kindness as strengths, encouraging a form of love that is nurturing and empathetic.

Balance and *Yin-Yang*

Love, like all things in Taoism, is about balance—the interplay of *yin* (passive, receptive energy) and *yang* (active, assertive energy).

A Taoist perspective on love acknowledges both the softness and strength within relationships, recognising that harmony comes from the balance of opposites rather than dominance or submission.

Detachment and Non-Possessiveness

Taoist love does not cling or possess. It encourages a form of love that is free from attachment and selfish desire, echoing the broader Taoist principle of non-attachment to material or emotional states.

This is not to be mistaken for indifference, but rather a love that respects freedom, individuality, and the natural flow of life.

Interconnectedness

Love in Taoism is not confined to human relationships but extends to all beings and nature itself. The Taoist concept of love embraces a deep connection with the world, reflecting the belief that all things are part of a single, unified whole.

Self-Love and Inner Peace

Taoism encourages self-cultivation and inner harmony.

By being in tune with the Tao, one fosters love not just externally but internally, which radiates naturally in interactions with others.

In essence, Taoist love is a reflection of the Tao: fluid, humble, compassionate, and balanced, emphasising natural harmony over artificial constructs or intense passions. It invites individuals to love freely, gently, and without conditions, mirroring the effortless flow of the universe itself.

III.5 Love in Confucianism

In Confucianism, the concept of love is complex and multifaceted, rooted in social relationships, moral cultivation, and the broader aim of social harmony. The most relevant term associated with love in Confucian thought is *Ren,* often translated as benevolence, humaneness, or compassion.

Ren: The Foundation of Love

Ren is the highest virtue in Confucian ethics, representing an all-encompassing love and concern for others.

It embodies empathy, kindness, and care, not as an abstract feeling but as an active commitment to moral behaviour and social responsibility.

Confucius described a person with *Ren* as someone who seeks to establish others when establishing oneself and to help others reach their goals while achieving one's own.

Love in Hierarchical Relationships *(Five Relationships)*

Confucian love is often contextualised within the *Five Key Relationships*:

Ruler and Subject – Loyalty and benevolence

Parent and Child – Filial piety and parental love

Husband and Wife – Fidelity and mutual respect

Elder Sibling and Younger Sibling – Respect and care

Friend and Friend – Trust and sincerity

Each relationship prescribes a form of love appropriate to the roles involved. For example, a parent's love for their child is nurturing and unconditional, while a child's love is expressed through filial piety and obedience.

Filial Piety: Love for Family

Filial piety is one of the most fundamental expressions of love in Confucianism.

It emphasises respect, obedience, and care for one's parents and ancestors, extending beyond individual affection to include ritual practices like ancestor worship.

The family serves as the training ground for broader social virtues; love for one's family is the foundation for extending love to the community and the world.

From Partial Love to Universal Love

While Confucianism emphasises love within close relationships, it also encourages the cultivation of love that extends outward.

Confucius believed that starting from love for one's family, one should gradually extend care to neighbours, society, and ultimately, all humanity.

However, this is a graded love rather than the universal love advocated by the Mohist school. Confucianism prioritises close relationships first but encourages their influence to ripple outward.

Moral Development and Love

Love in Confucianism is not just an emotional state but a virtue developed through continuous self-cultivation.

Through practices like rituals and study, individuals refine their sense of empathy, duty, and affection, transforming themselves into morally upright people capable of genuine love for others.

Chapter IV: Love in Modern Eastern Philosophy

Many modern Indian thinkers, such as Sri Aurobindo and Swami Vivekananda, emphasise love as both a personal and divine experience.

The fusion of spiritual and romantic love is evident in modern Hindu movements, where love is seen as a path to self-realisation.

Modern non-dual philosophies—voiced through sages like Ramana Maharshi, Nisargadatta Maharaj, and the Zen masters—often speak of love not as a fleeting emotion, but as the very pulse of reality.

Love, in this view, is:

The spontaneous fragrance of oneness—when the brittle illusion of separateness crumbles, what remains isn't an emotion but an open, effortless radiance. Love flows not as something done, but as something that is, naturally and without agenda.

Not a wave in the sea, but the sea itself—not a movement within consciousness, but consciousness unfiltered. It is the still, silent ground from which all arises and into which all dissolves.

This love is:

Beyond name, form, and self-concept—it cannot be possessed,

defined, or directed. It is prior to identity, untouched by ego's grasping.

Alive in stillness, found not in noise or drama but in presence itself—in the deep meeting of eye and heart, in the quiet recognition that nothing separates you from anything else.

It is not love for something, but love as everything. The rise of global yoga and mindfulness movements has spread these ideas to the West, blending spirituality with emotional well-being.

IV.1 Love by Sri Aurobindo (d. 1950)

Sri Aurobindo's concept of love is deeply spiritual, expansive, and transcendent. For him, love is not just an emotion or a personal relationship; it is a divine force that originates from the Supreme and helps the soul evolve toward union with the Divine.

Divine Origin of Love

Sri Aurobindo believed that true love is not of the ego but has its source in the Divine consciousness. It is the power of the Divine to unite all beings and draw them toward the realisation of Oneness. What we often experience as human love is just a reflection or shadow of this higher, purer, unconditional Divine Love.

"Love is the key to open the doors of the spirit."

Love as a Transformative Power

Love, for Sri Aurobindo, is not merely sentimental. It is a force of transformation. Through love, the human being is uplifted from ordinary, limited existence to a higher, spiritual state. When love is turned toward the Divine, it becomes a *bhakti* (devotion) that purifies and transforms the nature, removing ego, desire, and attachment.

From Human Love to Divine Love

Sri Aurobindo acknowledged that human love often begins with attraction, desire, and possession, but these are distortions caused by the ego and ignorance. True love seeks self-giving and union, not ownership. The evolution of love involves moving:

From desire to selflessness.

From possession to freedom.

From exclusivity to universality.

From emotional turbulence to peaceful joy.

Love in Integral Yoga

In his yoga, love is central. It is not only about loving the Divine but allowing the Divine Love to flow through oneself toward others and the world. Love becomes a bridge between the human and the divine, filling life with harmony, beauty, and bliss.

"To be capable of love and of giving oneself without demand and without

condition, this is the essential thing." — The Mother (Sri Aurobindo's spiritual collaborator)

Love and Union

For Sri Aurobindo, love and union are inseparable. Love drives the soul to seek union with the Divine, and union with the Divine deepens the experience of love. It is *ananda* (bliss) — the ecstatic joy of being one with the Infinite.

IV.2 Love by Swami Vivekananda (d. 1902)

Swami Vivekananda spoke and wrote extensively on love, especially divine love, selfless service, and universal compassion. For Vivekananda, love was not merely an emotion but a transformative force that leads us toward realising the divine in all beings.

How to Develop Love According to Swami Vivekananda:

See God in Everyone

Vivekananda taught that every soul is potentially divine. The more we can see God in others, the easier it is to love them genuinely.

"Where can we go to find God if we cannot see Him in our own hearts

and in every living being?"

Cultivate Selfless Love

He emphasised that true love is unselfish, without expectation of return.

"It is love and love alone that I preach. Give up jealousy and conceit. Learn to work unitedly for others."

Serve Others

For Vivekananda, service is a practical expression of love. Serving the poor, the weak, and the suffering is worship of God.

"They alone live who live for others."

Remove Ego

Ego is the greatest obstacle to pure love. By reducing attachment to the self (or "I"-ness), love flows naturally.

"The moment I have realised God sitting in the temple of every human body, the moment I stand in reverence before every human being and see God in him—that moment I am free."

Practice Detachment

While love must be deep and sincere, it should not make us bound by unhealthy attachment. Love while knowing that all is transient, and hold on to the eternal essence behind the form.

"Detachment is not that you should own nothing, but that nothing should own you."

Expand Your Heart

Swami Vivekananda often encouraged people to broaden their circle of love from the individual to the family, from the family to the community, and finally to the whole world.

"Love is expansion, and selfishness is contraction."

Regular Spiritual Practice

Through meditation, prayer, and study of spiritual texts, the heart becomes pure, and love becomes more natural and unconditional.

IV.3 Love by Ramana Maharshi (d. 1950)

Ramana Maharshi had a very deep, non-dual understanding of love. According to him, true love isn't something that is developed or created—it is our natural state, inherent in the Self, which is pure being and pure awareness. Here's how love unfolds in his teachings:

Love as the Self

Ramana Maharshi taught that the Self is pure existence-consciousness-bliss. Love is a natural expression of this bliss.

"The Self is love; real love is the Self."

So rather than seeking love externally, the path is to turn inward through self-inquiry ("Who am I?") and realize that you are love itself.

Ego and Conditional Love

What we usually call "love" in the world is often entangled with attachment, desire, and ego. Ramana pointed out that these forms of love are limited and dualistic.

"If one's Self is realised, then love, which is its nature, envelops everything."

When the ego dissolves, so do boundaries between self and other, and then love becomes universal—not just for one person or group, but for all beings.

Bhakti (Devotion) and *Jnana* (Wisdom)

While Ramana is primarily associated with the path of knowledge *(jnana),* he often said that true knowledge and true devotion are not separate.

"In the end, the path of knowledge and the path of devotion merge."

So, love for God, Guru, or Self—when it is pure and selfless—leads to the same realisation as self-inquiry. Love becomes a powerful force that draws the mind inward.

How to "Develop" Love in Practice

While he says love is already your nature, you can cultivate an environment where it naturally reveals itself:

Practice Self-inquiry: "Who am I?" to dissolve the ego.

Meditate on the heart centre (Ramana located the spiritual heart slightly to the right of the chest).

Surrender to the Divine/Guru/Self.

Cultivate silence—inner and outer.

"Silence is the language of God. All else is poor translation."

You don't develop love as a separate individual. You remove the veils—ego, thoughts, desires—and realise love is what you already are.

IV.4 Love by Nisargadatta Maharaj (d. 1981)

Sri Nisargadatta Maharaj was one of the great Advaita (non-duality) teachers of the 20th century. His teachings revolve around Self-realisation, the dissolution of the ego, and the direct experience of one's true nature — which he often describes as pure awareness or the Absolute.

Nisargadatta Maharaj on Love: A Non-Dual Perspective

Love is not personal; it is Being itself

Nisargadatta often pointed out that what we commonly call "love" — attachment, desire, affection towards a person or object — is not true love. He emphasised that true love is not between two separate entities. It is the natural radiance of Being, the fragrance of the Self.

"Love says: 'I am everything.' Wisdom says: 'I am nothing.' Between the two, my life flows."

In this statement, he's pointing to the paradox of realisation — when the ego dissolves, what remains is both emptiness (nothing) and infinite fullness (everything). Love, in its highest sense, arises not from a sense of lack, but from the recognition of unity with all things.

True love is beyond the mind

He made a clear distinction between mental/emotional attachment and the impersonal love that flows from self-realisation. Personal love is often transactional and based on identification. But real love, according to him, arises spontaneously when one recognises the Self in all beings.

"When you know that you are neither body nor mind, but the witness of both, and you are free of desire and fear, you are fully loving without needing anyone to love."

Here, love is not a relationship. It is a state of being that radiates naturally when the mind's projections dissolve.

Love is the recognition of unity

For Nisargadatta, the essence of love lies in the understanding that there is no other. When duality disappears, what remains is the natural compassion, warmth, and intimacy of the Self with Itself — in all forms.

"The consciousness in you and the consciousness in me, apparently two, really one, seek unity and that is love."

This implies that love is not an emotion but a movement of Being toward Itself, a sort of cosmic self-embrace.

Desire is not love

He was also clear that what most people call "love" is often just desire or need. He encouraged seekers to investigate their attachments and see how much of it is motivated by fear, insecurity, or the search for pleasure.

"Don't pretend to love — love is not for the mind. You can't think love. You can't want love. Love is when you forget yourself."

This is powerful: when the ego fades, when there is no "me" to need or cling — what's left is unconditional love, not directed at any object, but emanating from Being itself.

IV.5 Love by the Zen Masters

The Zen perspective on love is subtle, profound, and very different from most Western or romantic notions. Zen doesn't focus on love as an emotion or possession but as a way of being, an expression of deep presence and interconnection. Here's a developed concept of love through the eyes of Zen masters:

Love in Zen: Presence Without Possession

Non-Attachment

Zen love is not about clinging or needing. The Zen masters teach that true love arises from non-attachment, not because we don't care, but because we care without trying to control. When we release our grip on the object of love, love becomes boundless, like space.

"To love without clinging is the highest form of love."

— Zen saying

Zen doesn't see love as a grasping at someone to fulfill a need. Instead, it's the clear seeing of another, without the distortion of self-interest.

Loving Through Awareness

Zen places immense value on mindfulness and awareness. To love someone in Zen is to truly see them — not your idea of them, not your projections, but their true nature, just as they are.

"When you love someone, the best thing you can offer is your presence. How can you love if you are not there?"

— Thích Nhất Hạnh

This kind of presence is not flashy or dramatic. It's quiet, attentive, and deeply respectful. It listens. It notices. It holds space.

No-Self, No-Other

At the core of Zen is the insight that the separation between self and other is an illusion. From this view, love is not from one person to another — it's the natural movement of life when the illusion of separateness falls away.

"You and I are not two."

— Zen expression of non-duality

In this realisation, compassion flows naturally. There's no "I love you" in the possessive sense — just love, as the basic energy of connection and being.

Compassion as Spontaneous Action

Zen masters don't theorise love — they live it. To them, love shows up as compassionate action without self-consciousness. A bowl of rice offered without words. A soft gaze in silence. Love in Zen is less about saying "I love you" and more about sweeping the floor so another doesn't slip.

"Before enlightenment, chop wood, carry water.

After enlightenment, chop wood, carry water — with love."

Love as Emptiness

Zen often talks about emptiness — not in a nihilistic way, but as a recognition that all things are impermanent, interdependent, and without fixed identity. From this groundless space, love blossoms freely.

"Love is not something you do. It is the space in which all things appear."

— Attributed to a Zen teacher

When we embrace emptiness, we let go of needing love to be a certain way. We let go of "forever" and instead bow to the preciousness of each moment.

Chapter V: Love in Ancient Arabic Philosophy

Several major Arabic philosophers engaged with the concept of love, linking it to cosmology, ethics, and metaphysics.

V.1 Love by Al-Kindī (d. 873)

Love as a Cosmic Force

Al-Kind often regarded as the "Philosopher of the Arabs," was a polymath who contributed to many fields, including philosophy, metaphysics, mathematics, and medicine. His thoughts on love are deeply influenced by Neoplatonism, Aristotelian philosophy, and Islamic thought.

Al-Kindī's Concept of Love

Al-Kindī did not write a dedicated treatise on love, but his philosophical framework allows for an interpretation of love as an intellectual and metaphysical phenomenon. His view of love can be understood through the following dimensions:

Love as Desire for Perfection

Al-Kindī, like Plato and later Islamic philosophers, sees love as a longing for the perfection of the soul. Love is not merely physical attraction but a deep desire to attain knowledge, truth, and ultimate unity with the divine. This reflects a Neoplatonic perspective, where love is a force that elevates the soul from material attachments to intellectual and spiritual realities.

In this sense, love is a form of intellectual longing that drives a person toward higher knowledge and wisdom.

The love of wisdom (philosophy) is an essential way to purify the soul and bring it closer to the truth.

True love is not carnal but intellectual and spiritual, aiming at harmony with the divine order.

Love and the Nature of the Soul

Al-Kindī, influenced by Aristotelian psychology, believes that the soul is distinct from the body and belongs to a higher realm. Love, therefore, is not merely a bodily sensation but something tied to the nature of the soul itself.

The soul naturally yearns for what it lacks, and love emerges as a pull toward what is good, true, and beautiful.

This is aligned with the idea that love is the movement of the soul towards what it perceives as perfection.

This perspective aligns with Islamic mysticism (Sufism), where love is often seen as the soul's longing for God.

Love as Cosmic Harmony

Al-Kindī, as a philosopher of the Brethren of Purity and early Islamic thought, was deeply concerned with the concept of harmony and unity in the universe. Love, in this framework, is a unifying force that binds creation together.

He believed that the cosmos is governed by a harmonious order, and love is the attraction that brings things together.

Love is a cosmic force that maintains the balance between opposites—much like the Pythagorean and Neoplatonic traditions describe.

This view anticipates later Islamic mystical (Sufi) interpretations of love, where love becomes a force that unites all existence with the divine.

Love and Knowledge

Al-Kindī emphasised the connection between love and knowledge. He saw the intellectual pursuit of truth as the highest form of love.

He believed that love for wisdom (philosophy) leads to a better understanding of reality.

The highest love is the love of God, which is achieved through intellectual and spiritual enlightenment.

This concept foreshadows the ideas of later Islamic philosophers and Sufi mystics, such as Avicenna, Al-Farabi, and Rumi, who saw love as the path to divine knowledge.

V.2 Love by Al-Farābī (d. 950)

Love and the Perfect Society

Al-Farb, one of the most influential Islamic philosophers of the medieval period, integrated the concept of love into his political philosophy. In his seminal work *al-Madīnah al-Fāḍilah (The Virtuous City),* he posited that love is the primary force that binds individuals together and fosters a well-ordered society. According to him, love is not merely an emotional or personal experience but a profound philosophical principle that guides human beings toward collective harmony and intellectual fulfilment.

Love as the Foundation of Society

Al-Farb viewed love as the motive for human cooperation and the essential glue that holds society together. In his vision of the perfect society, individuals are united by their shared pursuit of the Good, which he equated with ultimate truth and knowledge. Love, in this framework, functions as the force that compels individuals to seek wisdom, cultivate virtue, and work together for the common good. Without love, social cohesion would collapse, and people would be driven by selfish desires rather than the collective pursuit of a higher purpose.

Love and the Pursuit of Intellectual Perfection

At the core of Al-Farābī's philosophy is the belief that human beings should direct their love toward the Good, which is intrinsically linked to intellectual and moral perfection. He was deeply influenced by Neoplatonic thought, particularly the idea that ultimate happiness lies in the union with the Active Intellect, a concept of divine intelligence that transcends the material world. By cultivating knowledge, wisdom, and ethical conduct, individuals can ascend intellectually and spiritually, aligning themselves with the higher order of the universe.

This notion of love as an intellectual and spiritual pursuit distinguishes Al-Farābī's thought from purely emotional or romantic interpretations of love. He saw love as a rational and purposeful inclination toward perfection, where individuals strive to transcend their limitations and become more attuned to universal truths. This aligns with his broader vision of a hierarchical society in which the most enlightened individuals—philosopher-kings—guide others toward truth and virtue.

Love and Political Organisation

In *The Virtuous City,* Al-Farābī describes an ideal society governed by wisdom, justice, and a shared love for the common good. He contrasts this with corrupt societies, which are driven by ignorance, selfishness, and a lack of true understanding. The leader of the virtuous city must embody wisdom and moral excellence, guiding people through knowledge and ethical governance. The love of wisdom and virtue ensures that rulers govern with justice and that citizens cooperate harmoniously.

Moreover, Al-Farābī's emphasis on love extends to interpersonal relationships within the city. He believed that a truly virtuous society fosters mutual respect, kindness, and a sense of shared purpose among its members. When individuals love the Good and strive for intellectual enlightenment, they contribute to the flourishing of the entire community.

V.3 Love by Ibn Sīnā, (Avicenna, d. 1037)

Love as the Principle of Existence

Ibn Sīnā, one of the most influential philosophers and polymaths of the Islamic Golden Age, offered a profound metaphysical and psychological analysis of love *(al-'ishq)*. For Ibn Sīnā, love is not merely an emotional or psychological state but a fundamental principle that structures reality itself. His philosophy of love encompasses three key dimensions: ontological, divine, and human.

Ontological Love: Love as the Drive of Existence

Ibn Sīnā's philosophical system is deeply rooted in Neoplatonism and Aristotelian metaphysics, wherein existence is understood as a hierarchical emanation from the Necessary Being (God). He argued that love is the very force that sustains this emanation, as all beings strive for perfection and unity with their source. Love, in this sense, is an intrinsic inclination in all things, from the simplest natural bodies to the most advanced intellectual entities, propelling them toward their ultimate fulfilment.

According to Ibn Sīnā, every entity possesses an inherent desire to actualise its potential and attain perfection. This teleological drive, which he identifies as love, ensures the order and coherence of existence. Even inanimate objects and natural processes function in accordance with this principle, though in a manner that lacks self-awareness. Love, therefore, is not an accidental property of the world but its fundamental organising principle.

Divine Love: The Ultimate Attraction to the Necessary Being

For Ibn Sīnā, God is the ultimate source of love, the most perfect being whose existence is necessary and self-sufficient. All beings, knowingly or unknowingly, desire Him because He represents the highest reality and the ultimate good. This divine attraction functions as a metaphysical pull, drawing all things toward their fulfilment and perfection.

In his *al-Ishārāt wa al-Tanbīhāt (Pointers and Reminders)*, Ibn Sn describes the love of God as an irresistible force that governs the cosmos. Even celestial bodies and the intelligences that direct them move in accordance with love, seeking the divine. The more intellectually advanced a being is, the more consciously it partakes in this divine love. For **Ibn Sīnā**, the highest state of existence is one in which the intellect is fully oriented toward God, achieving a state of ultimate bliss and unity with the divine.

Human Love: The Journey from Physical to Spiritual Love

Ibn Sīnā recognised that love manifests in human experience in varying degrees and forms. At the most basic level, love can be a physical or sensual attraction *(eros),* a force that binds people together through desire and pleasure. However, he emphasised that love must transcend mere physicality to attain its highest form—intellectual and spiritual love.

True love, according to **Ibn Sīnā**, is directed toward the divine and is cultivated through knowledge and wisdom. Human beings, endowed with intellect and soul, have the capacity to refine their love from the material to the immaterial, from the transient to the eternal. The more a person purifies their love, the closer they come to God. This transformation requires moral and intellectual discipline, as well as the pursuit of truth and wisdom.

V.4 Love by Al-Jāhiz (d. 868)

Al-Jāhiz, one of the most influential prose writers of the early Abbasid period, developed several nuanced and original ideas across disciplines such as theology, biology, rhetoric, and sociology. When it comes to the concept of love, his treatment of the topic is particularly fascinating because of his rationalist and observational approach, infused with humour and wit.

Love as a Natural and Psychological Phenomenon

Al-Jāhiz, influenced by the Mu'tazilite rationalist tradition, approached love not just as a poetic or mystical ideal, but as a natural psychological response—an interaction between the soul, the senses, and the intellect. He viewed love as a reaction to beauty, which he often defined in terms of symmetry, proportion, and harmony.

"The heart responds to what the eye perceives; if the sight delights, love may arise."

He saw love as rooted in sensory perception (especially visual attraction), governed by human nature, and variable based on personal and social preferences.

Love and Reason

Unlike the later Sufi tradition, which often celebrated love as an irrational, divine madness, **Al-Jāhiz** viewed love as something explicable and often predictable. He argued that it could be analysed rationally, even if not entirely controlled.

In his book *Risālat al-Qiyān* (Epistle on Singing Girls), he writes about how charm, culture, and behaviour enhance love, suggesting that love can be cultivated through education and refinement, not just physical appearance.

Types and Causes of Love

Al-Jāhiz's observations are almost sociological in nature. He categorised love into different types based on its origins and motivations:

Love of form (appearance)

Love of character

Love of wit and eloquence

Love born of companionship or habit

He recognised that attraction could be irrational or purely instinctual but tried to trace its social and psychological causes, such as:

Mimicry (wanting what others admire),

The novelty of the beloved

The power of glances and gestures

Proximity and familiarity

Love and Language

As a master of Arabic prose, **Al-Jāhiz** was highly attuned to the power of eloquence, and he often argued that speech and wit could be just as seductive as physical beauty. In some of his essays, he describes lovers falling for others through their rhetoric, humour, or poetic ability.

This ties love closely to language and intellect, not just body and passion.

Humour and Irony

Al-Jāhiz often treated love with humorous detachment, mocking excessive romanticism or idealisation. He pointed out how love could lead to absurd, irrational behaviour—contradicting his own rationalist tendencies. But this irony was intentional: he wanted to show how complex and contradictory human nature could be.

V.5 Love by Ibn Hazm (d. 1064)

Ibn Hazm, a prominent Andalusian polymath, theologian, and poet, developed a profound and nuanced concept of love in his famous treatise *"Ṭawq al-Ḥamāmah"* (The Ring of the Dove). This work is not only one of the earliest and most important pieces of Arabic literature dedicated entirely to love, but it's also deeply philosophical and psychological in its approach.

Divine Origin of Love

Ibn Hazm saw love as something divinely inspired. He believed love is part of the natural order of creation and reflects the beauty and unity of the divine. In his view, love is not just a biological or emotional reaction but a spiritual and metaphysical phenomenon.

"Love is a union of souls in their original heavenly form."

This idea echoes Platonic thought but is grounded in Islamic metaphysics, particularly the notion that all souls come from a divine source.

Love as Recognition of the Soul

Ibn Hazm suggests that when two people fall in love, it's because their souls recognise each other. This concept draws from the idea of the pre-eternal covenant in Islamic thought, where souls had knowledge of each other before being embodied.

He argues that love can happen instantly because it's a remembrance of that original familiarity between souls.

Types of Love

In *The Ring of the Dove*, Ibn Hazm categorises love into different types and stages, including:

True Love (al-ḥubb al-ṣādiq): Pure, unselfish, and enduring. It transcends physical attraction and is grounded in spiritual affinity.

Passionate Love (ʿishq): More intense and consuming, often associated with longing, pain, and ecstasy.

Imagined or False Love: Love based on illusion or physical desire without deeper spiritual connection.

He warns that not all love is noble, and love driven by lust or vanity lacks the depth and purity of true love.

The Signs of Love

Ibn Hazm, drawing from observation and personal experience, lists various signs of love, such as:

Fixation on the beloved's words and movements

Sudden joy or despair based on the beloved's attention

Jealousy and fear of rivals

Emotional transformation and obsession

These are presented in a tender, poetic style, reflecting both deep emotional intelligence and literary grace.

Suffering in Love

Love, according to Ibn Hazm, is often accompanied by suffering, longing, and heartbreak. He does not romanticize pain but views it as part of love's transformative journey. Love can lead to both spiritual elevation and emotional devastation.

Yet, he maintains that this suffering is meaningful—it refines the soul and deepens one's humanity.

Ethics and Chastity

In line with his Islamic moral framework, Ibn Hazm upholds chastity and restraint in love. While he deeply empathises with lovers and their emotions, he consistently promotes virtue, fidelity, and honour.

Love must be contained within ethical bounds, and when fulfilled in marriage, it reaches its most harmonious form.

Love as a Mirror of Divine Beauty

Ultimately, Ibn Hazm sees love as a mirror of divine beauty. Through loving another, one glimpses the perfection and beauty that is a reflection of God's attributes. Thus, earthly love becomes a path to spiritual love, or love of the Divine.

V.6 Love by Ibn Rushd (Averroes, d. 1198)

Love and Rationalism

Ibn Rushd was a prominent Andalusian philosopher and jurist known for his extensive commentaries on Aristotle. His intellectual framework was deeply rooted in rationalism, which also shaped his perspective on love. Unlike the Sufi mystics of his time, who often viewed love as an ecstatic and divine experience leading to union with God, Ibn Rushd approached love through the lens of reason and human intellect.

For Ibn Rushd, love was not merely an emotional or mystical phenomenon but an intellectual pursuit closely tied to the quest for truth. He argued that true love, in its highest form, is the love of wisdom and knowledge. This perspective aligns with his Aristotelian influence, where the ultimate goal of human existence is the realisation of intellect and the pursuit of rational understanding. In this sense, love becomes an aspiration toward perfection—an effort to transcend mere physical or emotional attachments and align oneself with higher knowledge.

However, Ibn Rushd did not entirely dismiss the emotional or passionate aspects of love. He recognised that love plays a crucial role in human development and in fostering social and ethical bonds. He was critical of excessive mystical interpretations that detached love from rational inquiry, believing that such approaches could lead to irrationality and obscurantism. Instead, he viewed love as a natural inclination that, when guided by reason, contributes to moral and intellectual refinement.

In his broader philosophical works, Ibn Rushd also examined the role of love in ethics and politics. He suggested that love and friendship serve as essential foundations for a just society, as they promote harmony, cooperation, and mutual respect. This Aristotelian idea of *philia* (deep friendship or love rooted in virtue) resonated with his vision of a rational and well-ordered community.

Ultimately, Ibn Rushd's perspective on love exemplifies his commitment to rationalism. By grounding love in intellect rather than mere sentiment or mysticism, he reinforced the idea that human fulfilment comes from the pursuit of knowledge and wisdom. His approach offers a compelling synthesis of reason and emotion, advocating for a balanced understanding of love that acknowledges its role in both personal and societal development.

V.7 Love in Sufism: The Mystical Perspective

Sufi philosophers and poets offered a more spiritual and experiential understanding of love.

V.7.1 Love by Rabi'a al-Adawiyya (d. 801)

Rabi'a al-Adawiyya, an 8th-century Sufi mystic, is one of the most influential early figures in Islamic spirituality. She is best known for her teachings on divine love, emphasising pure and unconditional devotion to God without expectation of reward or fear of punishment. Unlike many religious perspectives that focus on seeking paradise or avoiding hell, Rabi'a's approach was rooted in the idea of loving God solely for His essence.

Her poetry and sayings reflect this deep, selfless love, often using passionate language that resembles romantic devotion. She famously said:

"O God! If I worship You for fear of Hell, burn me in Hell, and if I worship You in hope of Paradise, exclude me from Paradise. But if I worship You for Your own sake, do not withhold from me Your everlasting Beauty."

This radical notion of divine love influenced later Sufi thinkers and poets, such as Rumi and Hafiz, and remains a central theme in Sufi mysticism. Her teachings challenge believers to transcend transactional faith and embrace an intimate, heartfelt connection with the Divine.

V.7.2 Love by Ibn al-Farīd (d. 1235)

Ibn al-Farīd was a celebrated Sufi poet of the 12th century, known for his deeply mystical and lyrical *qasidas* (odes) that explore themes of divine love and spiritual ecstasy. His poetry is considered some of the finest in Arabic literature, often drawing comparisons to the works of Rūmī in Persian tradition.

Themes of Divine Love in Ibn al-Farīd's Poetry

Ibn al- Farīd's poetry focuses on divine love, portraying the soul's yearning for unity with God. His works are filled with passionate imagery, often likening spiritual intoxication to earthly wine, a common metaphor in Sufi poetry. This symbolises the loss of self in the overwhelming presence of the Divine.

One of his most famous works is *Al-Khamriyya* (The Wine Ode), in which he describes a mystical wine that intoxicates the soul with divine presence, a wine that preexisted creation itself. This poetic imagery was not about literal intoxication but a metaphor for the overwhelming love and awareness of God.

Another significant work is his *Nazm al-Sulūk* (Poem of the Way), a long, intricate poem that outlines the journey of the soul through various stages of spiritual realisation, culminating in complete union with the Divine.

V.7.3 Love by Rūmī (d. 1273)

Love as Divine Ecstasy

Jalāl al-Dīn Rūmī, the celebrated Persian Sufi poet, mystic, and philosopher, saw love as the most transformative force in human experience. For **Rūmī**, love was not merely an emotion but a spiritual fire that consumed the self, dissolving the ego and drawing the soul toward divine unity. In his vast collection of poetry, particularly in the *Maṣnavī-yi Maʿnavī* and the *Dīwān-e Shams-e Tabrīzī*, love emerges as the central path to transcendence.

Love as a Consuming Fire

Rūmī often likened love to fire, describing it as an all-consuming force that purges the soul of impurities. This metaphor underscores the idea that true love, in its divine form, is a process of purification. The ego, with its attachments and illusions, must be burned away to allow the soul to experience the ecstatic union with the Beloved—God. This is reflected in lines such as:

"I burned, and burned, and burned.

I thought I knew love, but I was far from it."

This burning is not a source of suffering but rather a necessary transformation, akin to the way gold is purified in fire. Love's pain is, in reality, the gateway to divine joy.

Love as a Path to the Divine

In **Rūmī**'s vision, love is not restricted to human affection; it is a divine force that pervades all existence. He saw human love as a reflection of the greater love between the soul and God. This perspective aligns with the Sufi concept of true love, which transcends worldly love and leads to spiritual awakening. Rūmī often used the imagery of the lover and the Beloved to illustrate this mystical longing:

"Lovers don't finally meet somewhere.

They're in each other all along."

Here, Rūmī suggests that love is not about seeking something external but realising the divine presence already within. This idea resonates deeply with the Sufi understanding of *tawḥīd* (oneness), where the separation between lover and Beloved is ultimately an illusion.

The Role of Music and Dance in Ecstatic Love

For Rūmī, love was not only expressed in words but also through movement and music. He is famously associated with the whirling dance of the Mevlevi Sufi order, where spinning in rhythmic motion symbolises the soul's journey toward divine union. The practice of *sama* (spiritual listening) involves poetry, music, and dance to induce a state of ecstatic love, mirroring the soul's longing for the Divine.

In one of his most famous verses, Rūmī describes this divine intoxication:

"Lose yourself completely,

return to the root of the root of your own soul."

This loss of self is the ultimate ecstasy, where the individual no longer perceives themselves as separate from God.

Through fire, longing, and ecstatic surrender, love becomes the bridge between the human and the divine—a timeless truth that remains at the heart of Rūmī's spiritual legacy.

"I died as a mineral and became a plant,

I died as a plant and rose to animal,

I died as animal and I was man.

Why should I fear? When was I less by dying?"

(Masnavi)

Love and the Unity of Being

Ibn 'Arabī, one of the most influential Sufi philosophers, profoundly shaped Islamic metaphysical and mystical thought through his doctrine of *Waḥdat al-Wujūd (the Unity of Being)*. At the heart of his philosophy lies the concept of *al-'ishq al-ilāhī* (divine love), which he saw as the ultimate force binding all existence to God. Love, in Ibn 'Arabī's understanding, is not merely an emotion but the very essence of being, revealing the interconnectedness of all things with the Divine.

Love as the Essence of Reality

Ibn 'Arabī famously declared, *"Love is my religion and my faith."* For him, love transcends religious boundaries and doctrinal limitations, embodying the universal force that unites the lover, the beloved, and love itself. He perceived love as the divine energy that animates creation, drawing all beings toward their ultimate source—God.

Love, in this sense, is a mode of divine self-disclosure. Since existence itself is a reflection of God's reality, every act of love is an unveiling of the Divine. In his seminal work, *Fusūs al-Hikam (The Bezels of Wisdom)*, Ibn 'Arab explores the idea that love is both the origin and purpose of creation. He interprets the famous *hadīth qudsī*, *"I was a hidden treasure, and I loved to be known, so I created creation in order to be known,"* as an affirmation that the cosmos was born out of divine love.

Waḥdat al-Wujūd: Love and the Unity of Being

The doctrine of *Waḥdat al-Wujūd (Unity of Being)* asserts that all existence is a manifestation of the one ultimate Reality—God. Ibn 'Arabī viewed the multiplicity of the world as an illusion, masking the fundamental oneness of existence. Love is the means by which the seeker pierces through this illusion, experiencing the divine presence within all things.

For Ibn 'Arabī, love dissolves the distinction between the lover and the beloved, leading to the state of *fanā'* (annihilation in God). This process is not annihilation in the sense of destruction but rather the realisation that the self has no independent existence apart from the Divine. As the lover progresses in spiritual understanding, they come to see that their love for anything—

whether a person, nature, or knowledge—is ultimately love for God.

The Journey of Love: From Separation to Union

Ibn ʿArabī described the spiritual journey as one of moving from the perception of separation to the realisation of unity. The human soul, caught in the illusion of duality, yearns for reunion with its divine origin. Love acts as the bridge between the apparent separation of the lover and the beloved, guiding the seeker back to the One. This journey involves three stages:

1. *ʿIshq (Passionate Love):* The seeker experiences an intense yearning for the Divine, often expressed through earthly love, which serves as a mirror reflecting divine beauty.

2. *Fanā' (Annihilation):* Through deepening love, the seeker gradually loses the sense of selfhood, merging into the divine presence.

3. *Baqā' (Subsistence in God):* Having annihilated their ego, the lover attains a state of permanent awareness of the Divine, living fully in the realisation of God's oneness.

Love Beyond Formal Religion

Ibn ʿArab's vision of love transcended religious and sectarian boundaries. He saw divine love as the underlying truth behind all religious traditions, stating:

"My heart has become capable of every form: it is a pasture for gazelles and a convent for Christian monks, A temple for idols and the Kaaba of the pilgrim, The tables of the Torah and the book of the Quran. I follow the religion of Love: whatever way Love's camels take, that is my religion and my faith."

This passage encapsulates his universalist perspective—he saw love as the ultimate guide, beyond dogma or theological divisions. For Ibn ʿArabī, all paths ultimately lead to the Divine, and love is the compass that ensures the seeker never strays from the Truth.

Chapter VI: Love in Modern Arabic philosophy

Modern Arabic philosophers have explored the concept of love from a variety of angles—existential, ethical, spiritual, and political—often bridging classical Islamic thought with contemporary philosophy.

VI.1 Love as Existential fulfilment

Modern Arab philosophers, especially post-20th century, engage existentialism not as an import but as a response to crisis: colonial rupture, identity loss, political disillusionment.

VI.1.1 Abdel Raḥmān Badawī (d. 2002)

One of the pioneers of existentialism in the Arab world, Badawī saw love as a central part of authentic existence. He believed that love involves recognition of the other's freedom and a deep sense of responsibility, echoing Sartre but within an Arab cultural framework. Love, to him, was a way to transcend alienation in the modern world.

VI.2 Love and Ethical Responsibility

VI.2.1 Tāha ᶜAbdurraḥmān (1944-)

Tāha ᶜAbdurraḥmān, a prominent Moroccan philosopher, integrates Islamic ethical and spiritual traditions with modern philosophical discourse. His concept of love is deeply rooted in the Islamic spiritual tradition, particularly in the framework of ethical action, divine presence, and the development of the self.

Love as an Ethical-Spiritual Force

For Tāha ᶜAbdurraḥmān, love is not just an emotion or sentiment — it's an ethical-spiritual power that transforms the self. It is a core dimension of ethical subjectivity, meaning that to be truly ethical, one must be capable of love.

He critiques modern secular ethics for being too focused on reason and external action, and instead argues that ethical behaviour must be rooted in love, particularly love for God and for others as a manifestation of divine presence.

Divine Love *(al-ḥubb al-ilāhī)*

In his view, the highest form of love is love for God. This divine love is not abstract — it is manifested in action: in worship, in service to others, in self-purification.

This echoes traditional Sufi ideas, but **Tāha** integrates it with contemporary moral philosophy by arguing that true autonomy and ethical maturity come from aligning the will with divine love, not just through rational deliberation.

Love and Language

Tāha is known for his concept of "trusteeship ethics" *(al-amāna),* where human beings are seen as trustees *(amānāʾ)* of language, reason, and moral responsibility.

He argues that love reconfigures how we use language: not as a tool of domination or self-assertion, but as a form of service, compassion, and truth-telling. Love shapes the way we speak, listen, and relate.

Love vs. Utility

He strongly critiques the Western secular tendency to reduce relationships to utility, interest, or contract. In contrast, he says that love introduces a dimension of gift and grace, where the other is not approached for what they can offer, but for who they are in their divine essence.

Ethics of Proximity and Presence

Love, for ʿAbdurraḥmān, creates closeness *(taqarrub)* — to God and to fellow human beings. This "proximity" is both spiritual and practical. It means being fully present, taking moral responsibility, and refusing to let others become mere abstractions or means to an end.

VI.3 Love as Resistance and Identity

VI.3.1 Moḥammed ʿAbed al-Jabrī (d. 2010)

Moḥammed ʿAbed al-Jabrī was a prominent Moroccan philosopher and intellectual known for his critical approach to Arab-Islamic thought. While he did not write extensively on "love" in the romantic or purely emotional sense, his broader philosophical framework does touch on the concept of love, especially through his analysis of reason, ethics, and values in Arab-Islamic philosophy.

Foundations: Love and Reason

Al-Jabrī's most famous for his critique of the Arab intellectual heritage, particularly in his work *Critique of Arab Reason (Naqd al-ʿAql al-ʿArabī)*. He categorises Arab-Islamic thought into three systems of knowledge:

Textual: Rooted in language and religious texts.

Gnostic/Mystical: Based on intuition and inner knowledge (e.g., Sufism).

Demonstrative/Rational: Rooted in logic and philosophy (e.g., Aristotelian influence).

When it comes to love, **Al-Jabrī** is critical of the mystical or metaphysical system, which often expresses love as a mystical union with the divine (as seen in Sufi traditions like those of **Ibn ᶜArabī** or **Rūmī**). **Al-Jabrī** saw this system as encouraging passivity and escapism in Muslim societies, diverting attention from rational, concrete engagement with reality.

Thus, for **Al-Jabrī**, true love must be grounded in reason and ethics, not in mysticism or metaphysical speculation.

Ethical Love and Social Commitment

In **Al-Jabrī**'s ethical thought, love takes on a moral and social dimension. Influenced by Enlightenment rationalism and Islamic ethical traditions, **Al-Jabrī** would argue that love should express itself through:

Justice and fairness in human relationships

Social solidarity and responsibility

Love of knowledge and truth

Commitment to reform and rational progress

He saw the ethical reconstruction of Arab thought as a necessary foundation for love to be meaningful—not as mere passion, but as committed, conscious care for others and for the collective good.

Critique of Sufi Love

Al-Jabrī's view of mystical love *('ishq or maḥabba)* as found in Sufism is nuanced. While he acknowledged its cultural and poetic richness, he critiqued it philosophically and politically. He believed that excessive emphasis on divine love led to:

Neglect of worldly responsibilities

Devaluation of rational inquiry

Political stagnation due to fatalism or quietism

Thus, while Sufi love aims for union with the divine, al-Jabri emphasised love grounded in reason, ethics, and rational engagement with the world.

Love as a Form of Liberation

In his broader project of *tajdīd* (renewal), Al-Jabrī called for the liberation of Arab reason. Love, in this context, is not only emotional or spiritual but also a force for liberation and renewal. Love for freedom, justice, and truth becomes a driving force for reform, especially in a context where dogmatism and authoritarianism have hindered progress.

VI.3 Love and the Crisis of Meaning

VI.3.1 Nasr Abu Zayd (d. 2010)

Nasr Abu Zayd, an Egyptian Qur'anic scholar and thinker, is best known for his critical and humanistic approach to interpreting Islamic texts. Central to his thought is the idea that the Qur'an must be understood as a dynamic, living discourse, deeply connected to the historical and social contexts in which it is read. Within this broader interpretive framework, love emerges not merely as an emotional or personal state but as a spiritual, ethical, and social principle.

Love as Divine Attribute and Human Calling

Abu Zayd emphasised that God's love is an essential attribute in the Qur'an. Although not one of the "99 Names of God," love is described as one of God's acts and orientations:

"Indeed, Allah loves those who do good (muḥsinīn)." (Qur'an 2:195)

This divine love is not unconditional—rather, it is connected to moral and ethical behaviour. For Abu Zayd, this reveals that love in the Qur'an is relational and ethical. It is a two-way relationship: God's love must be reciprocated through just action, compassion, and striving for good.

Thus, love becomes a moral compass for human beings. Loving God means engaging in the ethical life—promoting justice, mercy, and care for others.

Love as Interpretation: The Hermeneutics of Compassion

At the heart of Abu Zayd's methodology is hermeneutics—the art of interpretation. He saw the Qur'an not as a static text with fixed meanings but as a dynamic dialogue between text and reader.

In this dialogical relationship, love plays a central role. The act of interpretation, for Abu Zayd, should be grounded in compassion and empathy, not fear or rigid dogma. Just as God relates to humanity with mercy *(raḥma),* so too must humans read and apply the Qur'an with a loving heart that respects plurality and human dignity.

Interpretation is an ethical act. Love, for Abu Zayd, is part of that ethical posture.

Critique of Literalism and the Role of Love

Abu Zayd was a strong critic of literalist and legalistic interpretations of Islam that neglect the humanistic dimensions of the Qur'an. He believed such interpretations reduce the religion to a set of rules and overlook the spirit of *rahma* (mercy), *ḥubb* (love), and *ta'āruf* (mutual knowing).

In this context, love is a counterbalance to authoritarianism. It represents the humanising impulse within Islam—calling for a return to the Qur'an's ethical core. True religiosity, in his view, must be animated by love, not by coercion or fear.

Love and Human Freedom

For Abu Zayd, love cannot exist without freedom. He believed in the freedom of interpretation, speech, and belief. Just as divine love respects human agency, so must society. He argued for a pluralistic and inclusive understanding of Islam—where love is expressed through tolerance, justice, and open intellectual engagement.

In this way, love is linked to liberation—of the mind, of society, and of religion itself from rigid orthodoxy.

Love as Resistance and Reform

In Abu Zayd's personal life and intellectual struggle—especially as he was declared an apostate and forced into exile—love also becomes a form of resistance. His commitment to truth, justice, and the dignity of the individual can be seen as rooted in a deep love for Islam and humanity.

To love, in this context, is to struggle for reform—to revive the ethical spirit of the Qur'an and to challenge injustice, whether religious or political.

VI.4 Love as Mystical Unity

VI.4.1 Adonis (Ali Ahmad Said Esber, b. 1930)

The concept of love in the poetry of Adonis is deeply philosophical, symbolic, and often revolutionary. Adonis, a Syrian-Lebanese poet and one of the most influential figures in modern Arabic poetry, explores love not just as an emotional experience but as a force of transformation—personal, cultural, and cosmic.

Love as a Metaphysical Force

In Adonis's poetry, love transcends physical attraction or romantic sentiment. It often merges with cosmic and divine elements, representing a bridge between the human and the infinite. Love is a kind of existential yearning, an impulse to dissolve boundaries and touch something beyond the self.

"Love is not a meeting of bodies but a melting of souls into the eternal."

Love and Rebellion

Adonis views love as an act of rebellion—against tradition, against stagnation, and against the status quo. Just as he pushes for a renewal of Arabic language and thought, love in his poetry becomes a subversive energy, capable of reshaping identity and society.

"Love is not comfort—it is a revolution of the self."

Love and the Self

In Adonis's work, love is often introspective. He explores how love forces us to confront our inner contradictions, desires, and illusions. It's a means of self-discovery and self-destruction, a paradox that reveals truth through suffering and longing.

"I searched for you in me—and lost both of us."

Love and Language

Adonis is known for his linguistic experimentation. His treatment of love reflects this: he often uses surreal imagery, symbolism, and mythological allusions to describe love, portraying it as a mystery that cannot be pinned down by rational thought or conventional words.

"Love is the language that escapes language."

Love and Time

In his poems, love is both eternal and ephemeral—something that exists outside of time yet is deeply affected by it. He reflects on the impermanence of love, its fragility in the face of time, but also its timeless essence.

"I touched you in a moment—and lived a thousand lives."

VI.4.2 Khalil Gibran

Khalil Gibran's concept of love—especially as expressed in *The Prophet*—is profound, spiritual, and at times, paradoxical. His portrayal of love blends mysticism, pain, beauty, and surrender.

Love in the Eyes of Khalil Gibran

Khalil Gibran views love not merely as an emotion or a relationship between people, but as a divine force—one that elevates, transforms, and purifies. He speaks of love with a kind of reverence that treats it as both a gift and a test, something that brings both joy and suffering.

Love as a Sacred Calling

In *The Prophet,* Gibran writes:

"When love beckons to you, follow him,

Though his ways are hard and steep."

Here, love is portrayed as a calling—a higher path that demands surrender and courage. To follow love is to accept both its light and its shadow. Gibran warns that love will "wound" as well as "crown" you, emphasising that true love isn't about comfort—it's about transformation.

Love's Dual Nature: Joy and Suffering

One of Gibran's most enduring ideas is that love brings both ecstasy and pain, and that these cannot be separated:

"Even as he is for your growth so is he for your pruning."

Just as a gardener prunes a tree to help it grow stronger and bear better fruit, love also carves and shapes the soul, sometimes painfully, but always purposefully. This suffering is not senseless—it is a necessary part of becoming more fully oneself.

Selflessness and Freedom in Love

Gibran doesn't believe in love that binds or possesses. One of his most famous lines is:

"Let there be spaces in your togetherness,

And let the winds of the heavens dance between you."

Love, to him, thrives on freedom. It is not about ownership or merging into one indistinct entity. Instead, love is about two individuals standing side by side, growing like "two trees that grow not in each other's shadow."

This idea encourages respect for individuality within union—a kind of sacred distance that keeps love alive and breathing.

Love as a Teacher

Love, in Gibran's philosophy, is also a teacher:

"Love gives naught but itself and takes naught but from itself."

It teaches not by instruction, but by experience—by opening the heart, breaking it, healing it, and opening it again. Love teaches us humility, vulnerability, patience, and the beauty of giving without expectation.

Divine Reflection

Finally, Gibran often equates love with a divine force. In his vision, God is love and love is the way we experience the divine on earth. To love is to step into the eternal, to glimpse something far beyond the material world.

9 789198 945461